MW00852527

Across The Board

The Modern Architecture Behind an Effective Board of Directors

For Private, Public and Nonprofit Organizations

Mark A. Pfister

www.PfisterStrategy.com

M. A. Pfister Strategy Group, Inc.
P.O. Box 57
Port Jefferson, NY 11777
www.PfisterStrategy.com

© 2018 Mark A. Pfister. All rights reserved.

www.PfisterStrategy.com

No part of this book may be reproduced, stored in a retrieval system or transmitted by any means without the written permission of the author.

Because of the dynamic nature of the Internet, any web addresses or links contained in this book may have changed since publication and may no longer be valid.

Cover Design: Paul Roesch, Tupee Studios

Cover Picture: © VectorStock – expanded license - https://www.vectorstock.com/royalty-free-vector/simulating-engineering-blueprint-vector-221224

ISBN-13: 978-0-692-06426-9

DEDICATION

To all who said *'yes,'*
To all who said *'no,'*
And to all who continue to *'dream,'*
Profusely…

CONTENTS

ABOUT THE AUTHOR

In addition to serving on numerous Boards, **Mark A. Pfister** is a *'Board Macro-Influencer,'* a certified Board Director, and advises public, private, and nonprofit Boards in efficient and effective operations. Known as *'The Board Architect,'* he is also the inventor of the *'Board as a Service'* (BaaS) engagement model and an expert project manager, frequently consulting on strategic global initiatives in their initiation and operational phases. Mr. Pfister is a master speaker and conducts national speaking tours, lectures, courses and seminars focused on effective leadership, strategy, Board architecture, Board candidacy, professional project /program management and entrepreneurship.

www.PfisterStrategy.com

Mark A. Pfister

FOREWORD

$E = MC^2$ was a powerful equation that brought order to the inter-relationship of mass and energy. It took one stroke from a genius to bring a higher-order perception of the relationship to practical terms – this after centuries of understanding the individual factors, but without a repeatable formula, or *'architecture,'* to bring predictability.

Boards are no different. We all understand the importance in the individual factors of our Board existence... good governance oversight, challenging and endorsing strategy, CEO selection, and the like. Now, in *'Across The Board,'* Mark A. Pfister decodes the underlying architecture and ties the foundational elements into a futuristic equation that can be effectively applied to create, or reinvigorate, tomorrow's Boards. There is no reason why our comprehension and picture of the future Board shouldn't be as energizing and impactful as Artificial Intelligence or the Internet-of-Things in terms of how they are furthering and enhancing our non-Board Director lives.

I was introduced to Mark by a mutual acquaintance who simply thought two people with a genuine interest in advancing the state of Board effectiveness should get together for dinner. There weren't enough napkins to scratch the comments, grasp the concepts or process the insight Mark brought to the conversation.

For three hours I lived the 2012 version of *'The Laffer Curve'* – scribbled napkins and all.

It's fitting that the challenge to author *'Across The Board'* be undertaken by a person who has dedicated a great portion of his very successful professional life to studying, challenging, understanding, hypothesizing, theorizing and *'bringing to market'* the insights that he uniquely has in creating a predictable Board effectiveness model. Mark's *'day job'* is pushing the envelope on Board governance, contributing on Boards, elevating Board candidates, advising on Board construction and guiding companies in strategic growth... but that understates his reputation as the inventor of the *'Board as a Service'* (BaaS) engagement model, leader of M. A. Pfister Strategy Group's advisory practice, his numerous National Speaking Tours (in 2017, Mark gave over 80 lectures across the country on Board topics engaging over 14,500 attendees), published articles, monthly newsletters, seminars, consulting engagements, reputation for being *'The Board Architect,'* and his passion for cars – both antique and modern supercars. Mark's 200 MPH+ escapades in his *'4-wheel rockets'* and his U.S. Merchant Marine background as an Engineering Officer, certified to operate ships of unlimited horsepower and unlimited tonnage on any ocean, are just additional unearthed mysteries on my journey with Mark. I personally associated with the *'high-speed thrill'* while reading the first draft of *'Across The Board,'* which I am very flattered Mark asked me to critique. That part was easy... and the napkin notes continued...

Each of us will have particular insights from Mark in *'Across the Board'* that will stop us in our tracks. For me, the simplest *'ah-ha'* moment was the realization that just about all Board topics have been covered in depth in numerous books and articles... except for Board *'foundational architecture'* principles, which have remained untouched, and hence, one of the key original-content aspects of Mark's work. A few of the many additional and personal *'ah-ha'* moments for me included:

- It takes work to build a new Board from scratch, but it takes <u>courage</u> to rebuild an existing one.

- In-person Board attendance is a must. Much of the communication is in body language... completely lost on a squawk box.

- Channeling Roy E. Disney - pick one day to make each and all business decisions in ten seconds, and do it 100% solely based on the company values. Witness what happens!

- Do you have *'generational diversity'* as well as an accurate picture of the *'generational makeup'* of your Board? For example, are you leveraging Generation X's highly-developed revenue generating skills?

- A success formula for founder/entrepreneur CEO-led Boards is to introduce the notion of elevating her or him to Chairperson (only) with stewardship of the entire lifecycle of CEO succession.

- The fascinating history of formal strategy and why it is important for all Board Directors to fully understand how, to-date, only three professions have truly benefited from its strategic application and directly influenced its evolution.

- As a Chairman, I'm thinking more about the mentioned concept of *'diversity of thought.'* I'm tempted in my lifetime to try building a Board that, in addition to modern skill makeup, recruits an *'Analyst,'* a *'Diplomat,'* a *'Sentinel,'* and an *'Explorer.'* How cool.

I hope you, too, enjoy the energetic style that Mark brings to this newest evolution of Board governance insight, as I did. *'Across The Board'* has re-doubled my conviction to doing everything in my power to ensure that as a Director, I am fully committed to bringing the power of the best Board architecture insights to our shareholders – directly through our Boards.

- Michael K. Lorelli
Executive Chairman, Rita's Italian Ices
President, PepsiCo (twice)
Private Equity Operating Partner

Mark A. Pfister

Part I

Mark A. Pfister

1 INTRODUCTION

"If I had asked people what they wanted, they would have said faster horses."

- Henry Ford

Purpose and Meaning

The term *'noses in, fingers out'* is a long-standing code of conduct for Boards and the organizations they serve. At its core, it means that Board Members should have their *'noses in'* the business to understand enough to provide savvy and relevant guidance, but their *'fingers out'* of the business so as not to undermine or derail management. Finding this balance for well-meaning Boards, or for individual Board Members, can be challenging. After all, how is it possible to give relevant guidance and advice without having some level of day-to-day involvement in the company? Without proper governance, strategy and reporting, this is a definitely a valid concern. Furthermore, without the proper structure or *'architecture'* of the Board, this challenge can be further exacerbated to the detriment of the company.

In order for Boards, and the organizations they serve, to reach the level of trust, effectiveness and operational excellence needed to excel, the *'Foundational Architecture of the Board'* must be solid and constructed properly.

Having attended countless lectures, seminars and panel discussions on the topic of Boards, almost all have centered around established, public company Board Members speaking about challenges, experiences and outcomes of decisions their collective Boards have been involved with. Existing books and instructional videos seemingly mimic this genre with the same focus, albeit with the infusion of regulatory requirements and other Board governance areas. Some books attempt to give instructions and direction on the makeup of a successful Board, but leave out the detailed architecture.

Even my formal education in Board operations had the very same myopic approach. Yes, this can be interesting, educational and entertaining (not to mention great networking with other attendees at in-person events and executive education courses), however, an area that seemingly has never been covered or is skipped over is the actual *'nuts & bolts'* foundational and architectural considerations of how to build a Board from scratch (nonprofit & private companies), or how to envision the rebuilding or evaluation of an existing, in-place Board (nonprofit, private companies and public companies). This has been the case over and over again - until now...

The purpose of this book is to educate, in easily-followed terms, the successful and implementable architecture at the foundation of all successful Boards in the private, public and nonprofit sectors – all the while empowering you with a simple roadmap to ensure success from the start.

Whether you are on an existing Board, plan on joining a Board, tasked with building or revamping a Board or simply interested in a way to further evaluate if a Board you might join will be successful, this methodology will be extremely useful to you.

Remember, building a Board from scratch, or rebuilding an existing Board, without consideration or evaluation of the most important foundational architectural elements will almost certainly lead to years of floundering and stagnation. Most companies can't afford the remedial time, nor the massive amount of effort, to have this happen. After all, isn't the purpose of a Board to elevate your organization from the start? If you are building a Board from scratch for your company, commit to making the effort to follow a strategy and a plan. If you are evaluating or rebuilding an existing Board, the same commitment applies. Always start with your Board's foundational architecture.

If we were to look at where the journey of reading this book will take you, Figure 1 shows that it is in the earliest moments and thoughts of creating a new Board for your company, or in the first moments of rethinking and restructuring your existing Board – essentially, focusing on the architecture.

Figure 1: Focus of Reading[1]

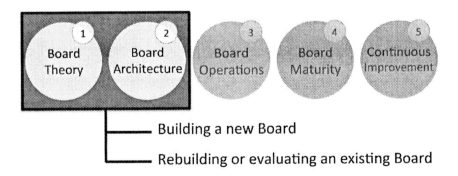

For clarity, this book will not go into depth on topics concentrating on Board operations, Board maturity or continuous improvement areas – those have been covered in countless available publications. For now, let's focus on the all-important Board foundational structure to ensure a solid base for you to build your Board operations upon. From my experience, this is and will remain the most important step... and remember throughout your reading, there is a successful formula and discipline to do this correctly! This structural discipline may come as a surprise to some in the nonprofit and private sectors, and potentially the public sector, where *'friends and family'* Board candidates can reign supreme, but you will feel knowledgeable and empowered once you know the in-depth thought process of the architectural formula.

Background & Understanding

We are currently living in extremely interesting times when it comes to the evolution of Boards and Board Directorship. The overlap between established, entrenched and accepted Board practices of old and the newer, more modern Board expectations have created somewhat polarized camps on the topic. Which side is correct and prudent? The truth is, they both are..., but the accelerating speed of change in this area is not easy. Change never has been easy. However, the discipline of Board Directorship and the dynamic environment that companies operate in today doesn't leave any room for a choice – it must change. It has to. The fate of Board evolution is sealed and the momentum has already started... and companies will demand change to stay relevant and competitive.

As a *'Board Macro-Influencer,'* I have personally advocated for many of these changes for the reasons of increasing the efficacy of existing Boards as well as promoting the next phase of the Board Directorship profession. This is a tall order in a somewhat secretive and impenetrable society, but a worthy one at that. My national speaking tours on these very topics have reached thousands and the seeds of change have been planted.

For the purposes of this book, you will witness that I sometimes don't differentiate between a Board of Directors and a Board of Advisors - or a working combination of the two. This is not by accident and it is not meant to confuse. By definition, a Board Advisor's job is to provide advice and counsel. A Board Director's job, by definition, is to provide governance, although I would vehemently add *strategy and strategic guidance* to the front of the responsibility list. It will ultimately be your decision on which designation and responsibilities you choose (director vs. advisor), as long as you are not under the umbrella of certain regulations, as a public company would be. The reason I don't differentiate the classification is simple. The modern foundational structure of your overall support team, by means of an effective Board, does not need to deviate from the proper expertise, experience and demeanor of your Board members, regardless of whether or not they are non-voting members or conversely, fiduciaries. For some experienced public Board Members reading this book, these comments likely will ring in their ears as blasphemy. This clarification on approach, first and foremost, is to allow for a laser-focus on the architecture and build of a modern and effective support team – regardless of a Board Member's formal designation as a voting or non-voting member. The details within this book will clarify and reinforce this approach.

For proper due-diligence, we should, however, initially define and clarify the main differences between a Board of Directors and a Board of Advisors.

Figure 2: Board of Directors vs. Board of Advisors[1]

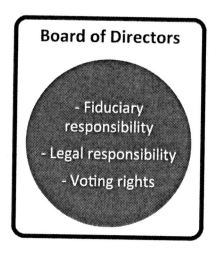

These are significant differences in having a true legal voice in final company decisions and outcomes, but once again, in my experience, the same outcomes can be achieved in a private or nonprofit organization where the final and counted *'vote'* is being made by informed and non-egotistical business leader(s).

Yes, there are some construction limitations when it comes to certain Boards with investor considerations in the private sector or shareholder / regulation considerations in the public sector, but don't let this cloud or divert the potential of basing your Board structure decision-making against a foundational strategic path and plan. It is possible to do this in all cases. No exceptions apply. In my experience as a Board Member, Board Advisor, executive coach and business strategist – involved with hundreds of Boards, Board Committees, Board Members and executives - I've yet to encounter a situation in which all, or the bulk of a strategic Board build or rebuild strategy / plan couldn't be achieved when there was total *'buy-in'* that a new approach or change was warranted. This is proof in the fact that with a conceptual roadmap covering the foundational architectural elements of your Board, you know definitively if you are on a successful path or not, right from the start – and will be able to make course corrections where and when it is appropriate on the journey.

All too often, the foundational architecture of the Board has been ignored. More so, there is little discussion or alignment on the existence of *'discipline'* around Board architecture, or even the view of the knowledge and experience of building a Board effectively as *'a discipline.'* The very utterance of this topic typically brings about confused looks when discussed in open forums. Why? Because many believe that Boards simply exist to bring credibility via famous names to the organization. Then, it is believed, a further network of connections through this *'famous'* name can be leveraged for the organization's benefit. Additionally, some nonprofits select Board Members simply based on the Board candidate's ability to cut a yearly check to the organization they serve. There is much more to this entire formula that many do not realize, or think about. They are not aware of the structural discipline behind successful Boards that make them truly efficient and effective.

In the public sector, we often see this lack of structural regard with the appointment of a high percentage of similar-background Board Members in a company or familiar and well-known business *'stars'* sitting on multiple Boards (and possibly too many Boards) simultaneously. Yes, this does not necessarily always manifest itself in a negative scenario in all cases, but it can drastically increase the risk of below-average performance due to lack of team diversity and potential time commitment constraints (a common term used for a Board Director spread thin across multiple organizations is called *'overboarding'*). As most financial investment firms list in their mouseprint, *"past performance is not indicative of future results."* This is true of Boards and Board Members, too. Now, in all fairness, the public sector has multiple additional regulations and mandates to ensure Board and company compliance, but once again, I believe these do not go far enough to give unequivocal guidance on foundational Board structuring and architectural theory to ensure company and shareholder success. Know that most Board compliance regulations in the public sector are working under the assumption that your Board is already structured properly and operating efficiently. As you may have guessed, this is typically not the case. A Board simply checking the boxes for regulatory compliance is far from creating effective and modern governance structures, or weighing in on ground-breaking business strategies.

In both the private and nonprofit sectors, we frequently also see a blatant disregard for Board structuring when sports stars are announced as Board Members of small and large organizations. Twenty years of sports stardom is undoubtedly no small feat, but just because you had a record breaking batting average, or you won the U.S. Open 10 times, by no means qualifies you to effectively manage your duties and responsibilities as a Board Member, or even a Board Advisor, of a company.

Although the example areas of credibility and a network of connections are undoubtedly important traits for a Board Member to bring to a company, it is by no means the sole or top evaluation criteria. When an amateur CEO and/or Chairperson speaks about a Board they plan on building for their private company, or one they have already put in place, they will typically only speak of the past accomplishments or *'fame'* of those involved Directors – which is an indirect way of saying that the main evaluation criteria for their Board Members' appointments were: a) their credibility from past experience, and b) their potential available network of connections. As we get further into this book, you will see where these important criteria fit into the bigger picture, but these are just a few of the many important Board build and evaluation considerations we will cover and prioritize.

Let's reference the nonprofit world, for a moment, as an example of rampant underestimation of Board Director and Board Advisor roles & responsibilities - it will help in also easily correlating parallels to the public and private sectors.

So as not to be labeled as insensitive, I will say first that I fundamentally and wholeheartedly believe that the world is a better place due to nonprofit organizations. Whether for scenarios involving social services, disaster relief & recovery, serving underprivileged portions of our population or simply furthering countless worthwhile causes, nonprofits have and continue to serve their purpose to elevate society…, but not without their significant challenges. Namely, the effectiveness and efficiency of their Boards, which ultimately challenges the ongoing success and longevity of the organizations they serve, not to mention the trust and confidence of the donating public. The research supports this;

In 2015, a survey of over 924 nonprofit Board Directors by the Stanford Graduate School of Business, in collaboration with BoardSource and GuideStar[2], focused on the 'composition, structure and practices of nonprofit organization Boards.' Some may consider the findings to be astounding. For others who have served on challenged nonprofit Boards, you will likely nod your head in agreement.

The study reported:

- *"The skills, resources, and experience of Directors are not sufficient to meet the needs of most nonprofit organizations."*

- Nonprofit *"Board processes fall short."*

- *"Over a quarter of nonprofit Directors do not have a deep understanding of the mission and strategy of their organization."*

- *"Nearly a third"* of nonprofit Directors *"are dissatisfied with the Board's ability to evaluate organizational performance."*

- *"A majority"* of nonprofit Directors *"do not believe their fellow Board Members are very experienced or engaged in their work."*

Furthermore, a 2016 study conducted by Concord Leadership Group in the nonprofit space[3] surfaced issues with the collective output of nonprofit Board action (or inaction):

- *"49 of 100 nonprofits"* surveyed *"are operating without a strategic plan."*

- *"77% of nonprofits have no succession plan or leadership development program,"* (even with the unprecedented Baby Boomer retirement currently in play).

- *"42% of nonprofits do not have any formal evaluation systems for anyone"* on the Board.

Wow! All of these major shortcomings reside in foundational areas that define an effective and efficient Board. So, where should nonprofit (as well as public and private) organizations focus their efforts to right these wrongs? The answer is surprisingly simple - implement formal Board structuring in the form of proper architecture, as well as formal evaluation processes, within their organizations.

Chairmen / Chairwomen need to have the courage and be willing to push structure and formality across the Boards they lead. Many Chairpersons in the private and nonprofit sectors have inherited Boards that were built solely on the *'friends and family'* candidate approach with little to no expectations, requirements or performance measurements. This typically doesn't last long and can (and likely will) jeopardize their organization's success. Questions for Chairpersons to ask their fellow Board members and plan for remediation when evaluating the buy-in, dedication and effectiveness of their team are many, but the following rise to the top.

Does your fellow Board Member:

- View their position as a true '*job*' with responsibilities?

- Have leadership, Board Director, Board Advisor and/or C-Level experience?

- Have formal training or certifications in the discipline of Board Directorship? (more on this later...)

- Have the time to dedicate and made the commitment to their role? (more on this in Chapter 13: '*Board Member Evaluation & Selection.*') In the meantime, make note:
  o I have never seen a truly successful Board Director dedicate less than 200+ hours per year per organization (public, private, or nonprofit). Supportive of this belief, a recent study by the National Association of Corporate Directors (NACD) puts the average public Board Director's yearly time commitment at 245-248 hours per year.[3a]
  o I have never seen a truly successful Board Advisor put in less than 50 hours per year per organization (public, private, or nonprofit)

- Know the organization's values, vision and mission by heart?

- When appropriate, spend time with the organization's operations staff to get first-hand information?

- When appropriate, get involved in the organization above and beyond Board Director duties?

- Attend Board meetings in person?

- Consistently attend Board meetings?

- Lead or get involved in Board committees?

- Submit or contribute to a monthly, or quarterly status report for their Board Committee?

- Assist in setting Board and organization performance expectations?

- Have the demeanor, emotional intelligence and mindfulness to foster an environment of trust and camaraderie with all Board Members?

Honest answers to these 13 questions can be quite insightful and allow for a transparent look into the organization. After all, the Board is the main launching point for the values, vision, and mission of the organization.

When it comes to nonprofits, notice how I failed to mention anything about the amount of revenue/donations a Board Director in a nonprofit can bring into the organization. This is not an oversight. Many times the nonprofit Director's ability to personally donate to the organization is the first (and only) deciding factor on their appointment to a nonprofit Board - and this is typically a big mistake. Where most nonprofits initially fail is either in their strategy, their governance, their operations, or all of these combined. There is usually not just one cause as a stand-alone flag, but a homogeneous mixture of shortcomings in all of these areas combined. These focus disciplines need to be paramount considerations for Board Director expertise. Truly successful nonprofit organizations incorporate their maximum donation outreach potential through their strategy on a macro level, not individual Board *'heroes'* at a micro level who write a yearly check. Yes, a common additional requirement of nonprofit Board directorship includes the ability to donate to the organization, but I will take a dedicated and disciplined Board Member, with the ability to generate donations through their network as well as through their succinct understanding of the organization's mission and strategy, over a *'hero'* Board Member with a checkbook, any day of the week.

Further Clarification

Let's now switch gears for a moment to the private sector where the changing roles & responsibilities of private company Board Directors have left some companies in a tailspin.

Privately held companies aren't mandated to have a Board. There are no stipulations or requirements that say they have to form a Board. There are no public reporting requirements that have to be met... So why form this team? What are the benefits to a private company? And what is the benefit to a private company Board Member? The answer is *'many.'*

The fact is, much has been learned and borrowed from the public Board sector and successfully applied in the private Board sector. Although private companies don't fall under the umbrella of Dodd Frank or Sarbanes-Oxley regulations, the ripple effect of these rules for public companies seeped into the culture and approach of private companies as well as their Boards. Turns out that the transparency, accountability, and other governance best-practices also could find a welcome home in non-regulated companies. This is a good trend.

It could be argued, conversely, that private company Board practices have made their way into the public sector, too. After all, the number of private company Board Directors that are now serving public company Boards in recent years has greatly increased as the massive baby-boomer retirement track heats up - allowing for private company Board Directors to have a shot in the public realm. Another good trend.

All of this said, the requirements and expectations of private company Board Directors have evolved and changed quite drastically over the past few years - more so than any regulation's or legislation's effect on Board members within the public sector in the same timeframe. Simply having a recognizable name and a successful track record are no longer enough (or even required in some cases) to ensure a seat at the private Board table. What matters most today is the private Board Director's ability to simultaneously promote meaningful action, foster accountability, convey trustworthiness, grow networks and provide mediation to the organization[4] - all without the rigid regulation structure and guardrails that public companies utilize to keep this transparent and in check. Simply showing up to a Board meeting and offering up un-researched advice definitely will not cut it any longer. Private Board Directors essentially have to operate with both 'sole proprietor' and 'team' culture characteristics to be successful - hence the lofty challenge for today's private company Board Directors to stay relevant and effective to the companies they serve. When each Board member is at this level, the entire Board is at this level... and that's a great benefit to both the private company and the private Board Director.

Trending & Statistics

Before we jump into the details of successful Board architecture, there is value in knowing the trending and metrics of certain

Board-related data points. After all, you don't know where you are going unless you know where you came from. This data and subsequent trending allows us to further predict the trajectory of the Board vertical, hence allowing us a unique view into where things are headed.

Boards look very different than they did a decade ago, according to Spencer Stuart's '2016 *Board Index of S&P 500 Companies*.'[5] This view of public company trending serves quite well as a bellwether for the entire Board Director profession and the companies they serve:

Figure 3: Board Trending[5]

	Trending	2016	2006
Average Board Size	↑	10.8	10.7
% Independent Directors	↑	85%	81%
CEO also serving as company Chairperson	↓	52%	67%
CEOs also serving on outside company Boards	↓	43%	55%
Mandatory retirement age requirement	↓	73%	78%
Retirement age of 75+	↑	39%	9%
Retirement age of 72+	↑	94%	57%
*Declassified Boards (one-year terms)	↑	95%	61%

'*Average Board size*' has increased in parallel to the '*percentage of Independent Directors.*' The '*CEO also serving as company Chairperson*' as well as the '*CEO also serving on outside company Boards*' has decreased. These trends are presumably based on the increasing responsibilities and requested dedication of the associated positions.

*Classified Boards, "*also colloquially known as staggered Boards,*

17

create separate 'classes' of directors who are elected for multiple-year terms, with one 'class' coming up for re-election each year. Proponents of classified Boards say they strengthen a company's long-term strategy by increasing focus and dedication. Classification may also reduce stress on a Board by creating job stability and preventing hostile corporate takeovers. On the other hand, advocates of declassified Boards highlight how annual elections can increase accountability and responsiveness to shareholders. Over the past five years, corporations have seen a strong migration away from classified Boards to annually elected [declassified] Boards with no director classes."[6]

Also, according to Spencer Stuart's '2016 Board Index of S&P 500 Companies,'[5] new Independent/Outside Directors look somewhat different than they did just 10 years earlier:

Figure 4: New Independent/Outside Directors[5]

	Trending	2016	2006
Active CEOs / COOs / Presidents	↓	19	29
Retired CEOs / COOs / Presidents	↑	19%	11%
Division or Subdivision President	↑	13%	5%
Functional Head	←→	10%	10%
Financial Background	←→	25%	24%
Academics / Nonprofit	↑	8%	4%
Consultant or Lawyers	↓	4%	7%

Once again, the C-Level/President trends are presumably based on the increasing responsibilities and requested unwavering dedication of the associated positions.

How public company Board Directors spend their time allows great insight into *'a day in the life'* of the position, too:

Figure 5: Board Director Time Percentage Allocations[5]

Attending Meetings	29%
Reviewing Reports	25%
Travel To/From Board Events	15%
Informal Meetings or Conversation with Management	12%
Director Education	8%
Representing Company At Public Events	3%
Other	8%

On average, 245-248 hours per year, roughly 4.5 - 5 hours per week, is what the time commitment breaks down to for public company Board Directors per organization they serve.[3a] If this seems like a large amount of time, that's because it is – and it is likely that it will increase more in coming years due to additional responsibilities, greater liabilities, increased shareholder pressure and fewer available CEOs. Incidentally, this increasing time requirement and expected commitment may have the effect of raising Board Director pay. Some believe that within the next few years, Board Director compensation packages could grow by 50% - 100% due to increasing demands, pressures and responsibilities on corporate Boards.[7]

Why all of the statistics and trending? In addition to the previous comment, *"you don't know where you are going unless you know where you came from,"* it makes you better prepared in your strategy and planning. As a Board Director, this should come naturally. I worry about Board Members who don't ask questions 80% of the time and offer advice, or guidance the other 20%. Data is your unwavering friend and deserves your utmost attention and respect.

Before we launch into the needed architecture considerations of your Board, let's align on a few definitions in this chapter to avoid having to break our flow in upcoming chapters:

- **Board of Directors, Board Director or Board Member**: A Board of Directors (B of D) is a group of individuals that are elected as, or elected to act as, representatives of the stockholders to establish corporate management related policies and to make decisions on major company issues (fiduciary responsibility). Every public company and nonprofit must have a Board of Directors. Private companies may opt to have a Board of Directors as well.[7a] (A 501(c)(3) organization must have at least one Director responsible for making strategic and financial decisions for the organization. Certain states may require a 501(c)(3) organization to select a minimum of three people to serve on the organization's Board of Directors).

- **Outside Director, Independent Director or Non-Executive Director**: Any member of a company's Board of Directors, with fiduciary responsibility, who is not an employee or stakeholder in the company. Outside Directors are typically paid an annual retainer fee in the form of cash, benefits and/or company stock. Corporate governance standards require public companies to have a certain number or percentage of Outside Directors on their Boards, as they are more likely to provide unbiased opinions.[7a]

- **Executive Director or Inside Director**: A Board Member who has the interest of major shareholders, officers, and employees (fiduciary) in mind and whose expertise in their business and their market adds value to the Board. They're not compensated for their position on the Board, as it is a responsibility of their job with the company. These inside

Board Members can be C-level executives, major share-holders or stakeholders such as union representatives.[7a]

- **Advisory Board, Board of Advisors or Board Advisor:** A group or individual providing non-binding strategic advice to the Board or management of a corporation, organization, or foundation (non-fiduciary). The informal nature of an Advisory Board can offer greater flexibility in structure and management compared to a Board of Directors. Unlike the Board of Directors, the Advisory Board does not have authority to vote on corporate matters or bear legal fiduciary responsibilities. Many new or small businesses choose to have Advisory Boards in order to benefit from the knowledge of others, without the expense or formality of a Board of Directors.[7b]

Ok. We are ready to get started... but if you haven't figured out the reason for the book's name, '*Across The Board*,' by now, this witticism alludes to the over-arching structure and architecture, across the foundational level, for a successful Board – and how it will springboard your company to a whole new level. In support of your implementation of a successful architecture supporting your effective Board, let's get started...

Board Fact: The first appearance of Boards of Directors in early American corporations can trace their roots back to similar provisions in English corporate charters. The 1694 charter of the Bank of England provides one of the best examples of English influence on American practice. The Bank of England's 1694 charter provided for a Board of 24 directors.[7c]

Mark A. Pfister

2 WHY CREATE YOUR BOARD?

"If you don't like change, you will like irrelevance even less."
- General Eric Shinseki

The topic of fostering a proactive and effective Board of Directors, or Board of Advisors environment has been a major point of discussion in recent years. I personally believe the reason for this exploding interest in the Board space is bigger than simply government regulations or the follow-on requirements of Sarbanes-Oxley or Dodd-Frank in the public space. Truth is, a large portion of Board topics and discussions have focused in the private and non-profit sectors. Twenty years ago this would have been a shocker as many private business owners would have asked the question, *"why should I create a board that could potentially add roadblocks in the form of documentation, requirements, over-structuring, bureaucracy or even red-tape?"* A valid question at the time.

Thankfully, the bulk of today's Board perceptions and value-adds in the private and non-profit sectors are of a different nature - and for the better. For example, the building of savvy Boards in the private sector are now viewed by some as a company '*getting serious*' and having '*arrived to the big leagues.*' Want your company to increase its growth? Build a Board. Want your company to create an industry-crushing strategy? Get a Board. Want your company to be viewed seriously for a capital raise? Create a Board. You get the picture.

Most CEOs, business owners and leaders are capable of driving the companies they lead to a certain level, but often become limited by lack of strategy and gaps in long-term planning - the curse of '*working in your business*' versus '*working on your business*' strikes once again. This trap, however, can be reversed with a savvy and functional Board...

Let's look at the granular reasons for considering the building of a board as well as the reasons for evaluating and potentially rebuilding your Board.

1. Boards Promote Meaningful Action

Figure 6:8

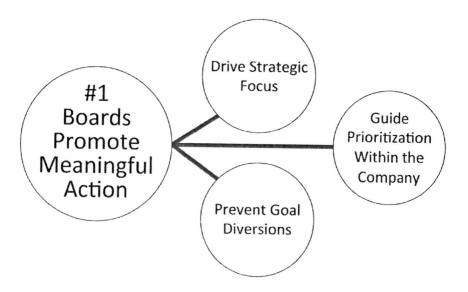

A properly structured and motivated Board has an uncanny ability to effectively promote meaningful action. This is not due to mandates or by demanding results, but more so for the three reasons of driving strategic focus, guiding prioritization within the company and preventing goal diversions. A Board that keeps these ideals in mind when guiding the company they serve can be quite effective and true to their mission. It should be noted that the most effective type of *'authority'* inherent in both individual Board Members as well as the collective Board is that of Charismatic Authority, not Traditional Authority or Rational-Legal Authority. For clarity, the definitions of each are supplied:[10]

- Traditional Authority: Power legitimized by respect for long-established cultural patterns (i.e. inherited, bloodline, religious, title, economic status, etc.)

- Charismatic Authority: Power legitimized by extra-ordinary personal abilities that inspire devotion and obedience (i.e. persuasiveness, transformational, elevate status quo, empower, etc.)

- Rational-Legal Authority: Also known as bureaucratic authority, is when power is legitimized by legally enacted rules and regulations such as governments (i.e. legal rationality, legal legitimacy, bureaucracy, etc.)

Board Members with Charismatic Authority are of utmost importance to the health of the Board and the company – we will discuss more on this topic in Chapter 13, *'Board Member Evaluation & Selection.'*

2. Boards Foster Accountability

Figure 7:[8]

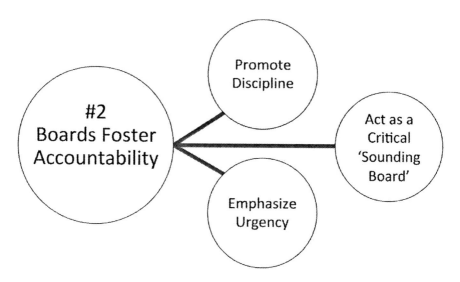

Accountability is another important trait that an involved and skilled Board brings to the table. CEOs of all organization types benefit greatly from a Board that is able to reinforce what is important, and in many cases critical, to the success of an organization. High levels of company-wide accountability can be achieved by a Board that promotes the need for discipline at all levels of the organization, acts as a critical sounding board on important topics & challenges and simultaneously emphasizes the urgency (and prioritization) of matters affecting the performance, viability, and reputation of the company.

3. Boards Convey Trustworthiness

Figure 8:[8]

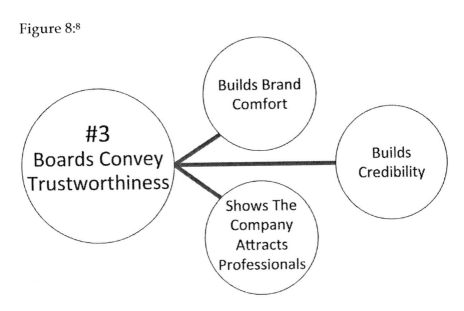

Trustworthiness, along with reputation, is an important consideration for all companies and it has a direct correlation to multiple critical areas, inclusive of sales. Trustworthiness with customers, associates, partners and stakeholders can be a main determining factor in the success of a company. Well-structured and smoothly-operating Boards can quickly elevate the credibility of a company allowing decisions by shareholders, investors, and even clients/customers to be made more easily, and more confidently. I can offer a first-hand experience in the private sector where the collective Board had cultivated and developed a high level of trustworthiness, thus bringing credibility to the organization it serves:

An early-stage private company where I served on the Board was in the throws of strategizing their capital raise approach. When the dust settled, we agreed that we would follow a path of debt financing first, then equity financing if needed. This particular business owner wanted more time to make the decision regarding offering up additional equity shares in the business until a later date, so debt financing was approached first through two channels - private financiers and formal banking institutions. The bank that was approached for debt financing had been affiliated with the business and the business owner for years, so the relationship and track record had already been established. The bank, however, took an interesting approach prior to final loan approval. Following the formal loan application submission, the bank requested to meet the Board! We of course obliged and it became clear that this savvy loan officer was sizing us up to assess the risk of repayment – she wanted to meet the team that was advising the business owner on how he would spend and invest that money. Our Board was not only able to establish trust and credibility through each individual member's experience and background, but also through the explanation of how the Board was foundationally structured to ensure the company's success. The architecture component deeply resonated with the loan officer. The stamp on the loan application said *'approved.'*

4. Boards Grow Networks

Figure 9:[8]

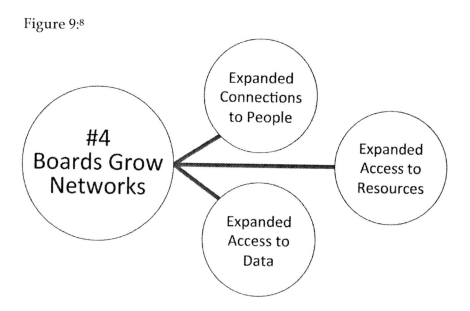

CEOs, especially when engaged within high-growth environments or organizations requiring business transformation, typically are not able to spend enough of the required time on the important aspects of growing their organization's network of connections... or cultivating existing in-place relationships. Fact is, the success of many businesses have been solidified by the CEO's presence in the proper networking and event settings. In today's world where CEOs are not only the public face of the organization, but also the protagonist of the show, the importance of high-profile face-time in the proper settings is very important. This is not always possible for some CEOs due to business needs and important commitments to drive the business operations forward. Boards have historically extended these networks, for both the CEO as well as the company, by multiplying the number of evangelists propelling the company's values, vision, and mission. Additionally, Board Members typically have the clout and implied authority to do this effectively for the organizations they represent.

5. Boards Provide Mediation

Figure 10:[8]

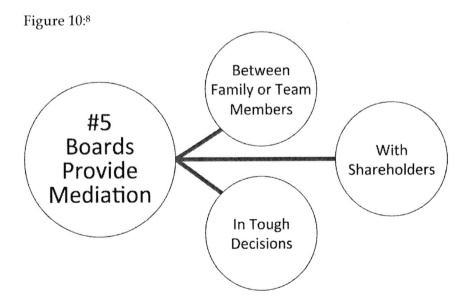

Mediation can be both a harsh word and a calming word depending on the situation to which it is applied. In tough decisions, with shareholders or between family/team members, it is wholly dependent on the situation at hand. In all cases, the outcome of a properly guided mediation can be very positive. Well-structured Boards are able to work through, or as Steve Karl, a professional colleague of mine calls it, *"lead through,"* any potential heated scenario that arises within the company to bring it to a beneficial conclusion.

Interestingly, when it comes to the topic of mediation, this has become a necessary skill for individual Board Members to hone, especially when applied to family businesses where succession planning is in play. Let's spend a moment on this important drill-down area as it deserves some attention and awareness.

For business owners in the private sector reaching or having recently reached retirement age, they are in the throws of the largest transfer of wealth in history thanks to their business success and the sheer size of the Baby Boomer generation. For up-and-coming business leaders, they are in the zone of opportunity to head these businesses in the near future... but, succession challenges loom with the prevalent belief that there are not many mitigation options to ensure a successful transition.

One challenging aspect of business succession includes the shear amount of data and *'local knowledge'* involved in a business transfer.

Another challenging aspect of business succession includes a very important decision - *'who'* takes on the company leadership role to ensure its longevity and success? Business owners have a unique, and somewhat challenging responsibility with succession planning. Many business owners feel forced into weighing the decision of whether to sell their business or transfer leadership to a designated family member successor. This decision is typically not an easy one due to concerns of dedication, focus and experience. Additionally, in scenarios where succession planning may include outside candidates, there are typically concerns regarding the level of business relationships and *'connections'* that will be required to benefit the business – after all, the business owner has built these relationships over a lifetime where he or she has been laser focused within their industry. In my strategy consulting, I have been asked by business owners many times which scenario makes more sense when applied to a family member succession decision: 1) sell the business and share the proceeds with their family members, or 2) turn over the business to a family member to run as a long-term *'annuity.'* Many business owners secretly lean towards the former as they don't believe their potential family-member successor has what it takes to keep the business afloat. This decision is even more nerve-racking based on the large amount of data available confirming *'less than one third of family businesses survive the transition from first to second generation ownership. Another 50% don't survive the transition from second to third generation.'*[11] These are not great odds and can do a disservice to a business owner's legacy; the importance they place on their legacy is something they may or may not admit to, but major concern for this is present in most cases.

There exists a third option, however, for business owners to get what they want with the confidence that their business will continue with a storied legacy when turned over to a family member successor or outside entity. This is where the Board mediation approach can be greatly leveraged. This third option sits nestled between the decision of selling the business outright vs. fully transferring the business to a family member or outside entity. This *'middle lane'* of thought suggests the forming a Board, or fortifying of an existing Board, in advance of succession, with the current CEO (owner) moving to the Chairperson position, to assist with the entire lifecycle of the transition as well as a longer-term strategic support mission:

- Pre-Transition: The Board, along with the to-be-appointed CEO, involved in detailed strategy, planning and preparation prior to the transfer of business leadership and ownership (...all the while, the Board acting as a needed mediator on terms, conditions and important considerations)

- Mid-Transition: Support, guidance and assistance during the transition per the strategy and outcome of the plan (...again, all the while, the Board acting as a needed mediator on terms, conditions and important considerations)

- Post-Transition: History and consistent advice/guidance for ongoing operations, challenges and future strategies (...and again, all the while, the Board acting as a needed mediator on terms, conditions and important considerations)

For a business owner, this offers up a unique and sometimes overlooked opportunity - pass the title and responsibility of CEO or President to their family-member successor and assume the role of a Board member, potentially the Chairperson, for a few years or more. I consistently recommend that all Board members commit to 200+ hours of dedicated time per year on their Board - this seems more than reasonable to most retiring business owners, who typically were working 60-80 hours per week, and also solidifies specific strategic responsibilities that are incredibly valuable to the company they started or have run for years. Likewise, successors experience elevated comfort levels in their new roles knowing that the transition wasn't a *one and done* event. For either a new leader or newly appointed position, having direct access to an involved member of the Board who happens to be the business founder or previous leader is an incredible asset sure to elevate the chances of long-term business success. With this model, across all decisions and strategic options, the Board can continually create a respectful and effective mediation outlet for all encountered issues.[12]

Trending & Statistics

Beyond the fact that public organizations legally require a Board, private companies (and we also could potentially make the correlation to nonprofit organizations) have statistics to prove that Boards indeed benefit a company's bottom line.

A survey conducted in 2016 showcasing the benefits of a formal Board in private-sector companies[13] highlighted some amazing and supportive results. Since forming a Board:

- *'87% of companies reported increased revenues'*

- *'82% of companies reported increased EBITDA'* - earnings before interest, taxes, depreciation and amortization

- *'Companies reported average revenue growth of ~48% since implementing their Board'*

Above and beyond the mentioned five granular reasons for considering the building of a board, or evaluating and potentially rebuilding your existing Board, these growth statistics provide further proof in the power of a properly structured and working Board.

Board Fact: Dating back to the 16th century, the term *'board'* was literally referring to the piece of wood that formed the table at which a council met. Over time, it also came to denote the meeting of this council seated at the table. In the early 17th century, the term *'board'* became synonymous with the group of people who met at the table. This is an example of a *'metonymy,'* a figure of speech in which something linked with a concept represents the concept itself. By extension, the term *'plank'* was used to describe a principle item of a policy or program.

3 WHEN TO CREATE, OR RECREATE YOUR BOARD

"It is never too early or too late to build or rebuild a Board for your company."

- Mark A. Pfister

To first cut to the chase, for public companies and nonprofits, this is not a choice – a Board is, of course, required by law. The question here would more so be *'if and when'* to rebuild the Board into a well-oiled machine that is continuously providing value to the company, as well as its stakeholders and shareholders. In regards to private organizations, they are not obligated to have a Board or Outside Directors, however, my simple answer to *'when you should create your formal Board'* is "*the earlier the better!*" If you are leading a private business, you may have to move somewhat outside of your comfort zone with this decision, but it will be well worth it.

I advocate for the formation of a Board at any stage of a business - from the one-person startup to the established, mature company. The earlier the better. After all, wouldn't you want the right strategy and support from the onset to ensure you are on the right path from the start? It could save you a lot of time and money. Too many private businesses think they need to be established first and then they will attract the right board members later - this is a flawed approach. If your company has detailed its value proposition and strategy along with compelling reasons for experienced Board members to join (i.e. great idea, challenge, performance-based compensation, aligned values, etc.), any company of any size can attract an extremely talented Board – either as Board Members or as Board Advisors (we will discuss further the topic of a *'Board Pitch Book'* to aid in this process in Chapter 13, *'Board Member Evaluation & Selection'*)

Removing yourself from the *'go-it-alone'* rigmarole and infusing focus into the strategic aspects of your business can reap huge rewards. Early stage companies may want to first consider building a Board of Advisors instead of a Board of Directors, as in most cases it offers more flexibility for the long term without sacrificing the critical guidance, insight and experience needed now. It also offers a chance to *'try out'* individuals for future consideration when you are ready to build your Board of Directors (know that this concept of *'trying out'* is controversial for some due to the belief that it diminishes initial commitment, but this can be alleviated with proper written engagement plans, a future Board Member compensation outline, and a timeline of the Board build structure). The importance of every person of your Board team being the perfect fit cannot be stressed enough – even one *'misfit'* can lower the overall effectiveness of the entire Board. Take the time to fully assess potential team members to avoid false starts which waste time and effort. We will review this point in detail in Chapter 13, *'Board Member Evaluation & Selection.'*

Most private companies aspire to be the next household name, so if you intend on raising capital or going public, forming a Board early gives you the opportunity to hone your team, improve your approach, and showcase your company before capital raises or an IPO. This will also positively influence potential investors and simultaneously build respect in your industry.

Board Fact: For some early-stage, private companies I have advised, in their first year of existence there were more Board Members & Board Advisors than company employees – these companies were being prepped correctly to be able to handle massive growth!

Mark A. Pfister

4 WHAT MAKES A GREAT BOARD?

"People are not your most important asset....the right people are."
- James C. Collins

What makes a great Board? This question is an extremely important one - after all, how can you build, rebuild, or lead a great Board without knowing what will make it great?

Over years of compiling simple, yet effective, reminders as I advise, coach and build Boards, I have my main *'go-to'* considerations that you can also use to kick-start and guide your thought process when building a Board, or evaluating an existing Board. You should also keep these in mind when reading Chapter 13, *'Board Member Evaluation & Selection,'* as they can be included in your *'Board Pitch Book'* when soliciting your savvy future Board Members and Board Advisors. Why? Because your solicitations should include the fact that you fully understand what is required for the Board as a whole to be successful... and you are also showing your potential Board candidate(s) that they have a great chance of joining a successful team.

4 Expectations of a Great Board

- **Remain primarily strategic**: Boards, in general, have a tough time with this concept. More specifically, a Board's individual members have a tough time with this concept. After all, if you randomly asked a group of 100 executives what it means to be strategic, you will likely get a large deviation of answers (more on the topic of strategy in Chapter 5, *'The Role of Strategy'*). For now, a simple, yet provocative, summary I can offer regarding a balance of time percentage dedication between strategic focus and tactical focus for a Board Member is the following: 90% strategic, 10% tactical. This seems to be the ideal balance. You may be wondering why exactly is there any commitment to areas that are deemed *'tactical'* for a Board Member, or a Board, to focus on – this would be a great question. The answer is that a percentage of time dedicated to the tactical components, most commonly through Board Committee work, allow a Board Member to be somewhat connected to the organization they serve, hence, making their strategy guidance and governance models much more relevant and effective. Caution should be taken to properly direct these tactical effort components so as not to breach the *'noses in, fingers out'* rule. Overall, do yourself a favor and remember this split of time. It will prove useful when evaluating your own actions and performance as a Board Member, as well as when evaluating other Board Members or your Board as a whole. Many symptoms of inefficient Boards can be pinpointed and corrected when focusing on this simple rule of thumb.

- **Keep the organization on track to its core Values, Vision, Mission & Credo**: Every decision a Board makes should be compared to the company's Values, Vision and Mission.

Seems simple enough. Shouldn't be hard to accomplish... but this is typically a recurring challenge for too many organizations. Most companies have a Mission (what they do well now) and many have a Vision (what they plan to be or enable in the future), but many organizations don't have documented Values and/or Values have not been properly infused or *'lived'* within the organization. The Board is responsible for the *'governance of Values'* in the organization. We will dive more deeply into these areas in Chapter 7, *'Evaluating Values, Vision & Mission.'*

- **Foster a clear and viable strategic company roadmap**: We often hear the term *'roadmap.'* It is actually so ubiquitous today that many confuse a roadmap with a plan or strategy. It is neither. The beauty of a roadmap is in its simplicity – the high-level steps required to a) drive the strategy, b) live the values, c) support the mission and d) reach the vision. Roadmaps are a Board's best friend as they allow for an easily referenceable checkpoint of actual outcomes – preferably with an associated milestone timeline. Roadmaps are often successfully leveraged not just at the Board level, but also at the organizational level through inclusion in company meetings, town halls and other progress-type updates. The clarity and transparency a roadmap can offer is extremely valuable.

- **Leverage knowledge and relationships to further the organization**: We like to believe that the Boards of all organizations would do whatever is possible to ensure success for the companies they serve. This typically is the case and I have personally witnessed some incredible dedication and selfless actions by Board Members on countless occasions. The effectiveness of this dedication, however, has an indisputable reliance on the knowledge, experience and relationships of the individual Board

Member. It is when the individual Board Members coalesce these qualities and traits with the entire Board, as well as the organization, that they reach a level of incredible momentum.

These four *'expectations of great Boards'* should not be underestimated. Their beauty and power is in their simplicity.

11 Traits of a Great Board:

- **Respectful = Constructive = Effective**: With respect, there can be constructive interactions that lead to effectiveness. Without respect, there cannot be constructiveness, which often leads directly to ineffectiveness. Respectful individuals achieve a lot, respectful teams achieve more. Now, this is not to say that disagreements can't be passionate as these typically arrive at new and better conclusions, but respectful disagreement is a much different game as compared to combative and belligerent disagreement. Some of the best performing companies in the world have highly-contentious Boards that consider *'respectful dissent'* as an obligation of the position. They do, however, always remain respectful to one another. Further to this point, there are also the important balance considerations consisting of overall intelligence (IQ), emotional intelligence (EQ), mindfulness intelligence (MQ), and team intelligence (TQ) in order for Board Members, and their collective Boards, to reach peak performance. We will go into more detail regarding these characterizations in Chapter 13, *'Board Member Evaluation & Selection.'*

- **Deep experience and focus on strategy and governance**: It is highly recommended that these be a requirement of every Board Member and Board Advisor. More candidly, for the Boards I build, this is an absolute requirement due to the fact that strategy and governance are the two most important characteristics for any and all Board Members, regardless of their industry or vertical knowledge. In Chapter 9, *'Infusing Planes of Congruence In Your Board Model,'* you will again see this recurring theme on the importance of every Board member having strategy and governance expertise.

- **Accountable and results-oriented**: When a Board, or Board Member is considered *'accountable,'* they must remember that someone else has been tasked with the *'responsibility'* for what the Board or Board Member is ultimately accountable for. That *'someone else'* with responsibility is typically the CEO and sometimes includes the CEO's immediate C-level direct reports. This differentiation between accountability and responsibility is important for a Board Director to always remember in all interactions as it will clarify areas of involvement and reach. In my Board work, I frequently create RACI charts, which are matrices of activities or decision-making authority matched to people or roles. At each point of activity, someone is assigned to be Responsible (R), Accountable (A), Consulted (C) or Informed (I) for that decision or activity. This structured thought-process at the Board-level is extremely useful in driving accountability to an outcome that is results-oriented.

- **Passionate about the company Values, Vision and Mission**: I will touch on the point of Values, Vision and Mission multiple times in this book. You have already read a short intro just a moment ago in the earlier section, *'4 Expectations of a Great Board'* under the second bullet item, *'Keep the organization on track to its core Values, Vision,*

Mission & Credo.' I will again touch on this important topic in Chapter 7, *'Evaluating Values, Vision & Mission.'* If you are sensing a huge importance that I put on this topic, you would be correct. Without spoiling Chapter 7, *'Evaluating Values, Vision and Mission,'* I will say that the company Values are likely the most important of the list, but more on that later. For now, remember that every Board Member must feel empowered, excited, and aligned to the company's Values, Vision and Mission. Without this dedication and passion, the Board is simply going through the motions.

- **Proper foundational structure of Board and Committees**: It goes without saying that the foundational architecture and structure of the overall Board is important – after all, that is the purpose and message of this book! Within the umbrella of the Board, however, is another layer of structure that ensures that the Board actually accomplishes what it sets out to do. This layer includes your Board Committees. Board Committees are where the *'actual work'* gets done within the Board and the importance of identifying and building your Board Committees properly carries much weight. Chapter 11, *'The Importance of Board Committees,'* will detail these considerations. The irony of this topic being discussed in *'Chapter 11,'* a common reference of the bankruptcy code, is not lost on me – but it is quite fitting to highlight a possible outcome when a Board and its Board Committees are not structured properly.

- **Entrepreneurial spirit**: There was a time when an *'entrepreneurial spirit'* was frowned upon within disciplined public Board circles. The very definition of being entrepreneurial included traits *'reserved only for private company Boards,'* definitely not for public company

Boards, where a more refined and corporate approach was the norm - and expected. After all, public Boards were teaching private Boards the ropes, right? The *'this is how its been done forever'* public Board rules were supposed to be the golden policies for any other *'lesser'* private company Board, no? Not so much any more. In actuality, it turned out there is an equal sharing of concepts and ideas between public and private Boards – in both directions... and you will now hear more frequently the request of public Boards looking for *'entrepreneurial'* candidates as they change their understanding of the true benefits to be leveraged from an entrepreneurial thought process.

Modern entrepreneurial Boards are now frequently described as *'progressive'* and considered a good thing in both the private and public sectors. A public Board *'progressive'*? Public Boards, and the companies they serve, historically have been accused of changing at a sloth's pace. How could such a previously entrenched belief seemingly be overturned in such a short amount of time? One reason can be chalked-up to the speed of change in every industry, regardless of business size. Some Boards proactively recognized the need for a more progressive thought process to stay relevant. Enter the entrepreneur. Another frequently undisclosed reason? Fear of disruption. The realization that a 2-person, entrepreneurial, private startup can become a major threat to a multi-national public company in a short amount of time has rattled many cages... and has forced the acceptance of a new entrepreneurial spirit in the boardroom.

Also, *"don't overlook private equity (PE) Boards"* when it comes to their entrepreneurial and progressive influence on Board norms, states Michael K. Lorelli, Executive Chairman at Rita's Italian Ices. *"The raw stats show 3,611 public companies in the U.S. vs. 16,800 private equity portfolio companies"* - the sheer volume of Board Directors in the PE space, along with their time-associated pressures on investment, cash-on-cash return and hold period, demand an entrepreneurial viewpoint.

Some public Boards still operate in the *'old-school'* bubble today, even when they somewhat realize that the survival of their company depends on *'entrepreneurial'* ideas and approaches, but changing the current culture is sometimes viewed as too large a feat to undertake, not to mention accomplish, in some companies. Avoiding this needed trait within a Board is a mistake and can prove costly. A key takeaway: know that extremely effective Boards, and the companies they serve, foster and build environments that equally share strategy, governance, and entrepreneurial-spirited approaches in the DNA of their culture.

- **Communication, communication, communication!:** A detailed study performed at MIT on the topic of communication found that *"...the key to high performance lay not in the content of a team's discussions, but in the manner in which [the team] was communicating."*[14] It was further confirmed that communication indeed plays a critical role in building successful teams. This shouldn't come as any major surprise, as it is typically witnessed that as the level of *'professional'* communication increases, the level of *'personal'* communication increases as well. Together, these communication interactions lead to strong team dynamics. High scores in the so-called *'sociometrics'* arena are important to note and are a paramount consideration for Boards to strive towards.

- **Culture of transparency**: Open and honest communication in any relationship is key. If, for any reason, you feel you cannot voice your opinion or disagreement for fear of reprisal or inaction, not only does the outcome of the topic become lessened, but the collective camaraderie of the Board becomes tainted, too. When transparency lacks within a Board, that Board is likely to experience offline lobbying, animosity and a general lack of trust between some or all Board Members – all are extremely undermining and detrimental to the mission of the Board. Fostering an inclusive and vocal environment is the secret weapon of many successful Boards.

- **In-person meeting attendance**: Reading body language – this is quickly becoming a forgotten skill for many due to changing work environments and the further acceptance of geographic flexibility. For groups such as Boards, who typically don't see each other on a daily or weekly basis, in-person meetings become even more important. A great approach for Board meetings is to cover both the professional aspect and the personal connection aspect. The Board meeting itself covers the professional aspect. A dinner of all Board Members can cover the personal connection aspect. Many Boards host the dinner the night of the Board Meeting – this is not my preference. I prefer the dinner to happen the night before to gel the personal connections and *'re-acquaintance'* prior to the Board meeting. The time to settle in, get down to business and quickly get to momentum in the Board meeting is drastically reduced and the meeting becomes much more focused.

- **Wide range of backgrounds, industries and expertise**: Variety is the spice of life. It can also be an accurate predictor of the future success of a Board and the company it serves. Why is this? How can someone from a different industry be key to furthering your company in your industry? Quite simply, it offers perspective... or, more accurately, a different perspective. I've served on Boards where marketing approaches from technology companies have been infused into the financial realm. Strategy components from pharmaceutical companies infused into the service-business realm. And the success has been incredible. Fresh perspective is the key. More on this in Chapter 9, *'Infusing Planes of Congruence In Your Board Model'*

- **Proper preparation for all Board meetings**: Last, but not least, by any means - come to Board meetings prepared! Overprepared if possible! I will admit that it sometimes tests my Emotional Intelligence (EQ) and Mindfulness Intelligence (MQ) when a fellow Board Member comes unprepared to a Board Meeting. This is not a common occurrence, thank goodness, for the Boards I advise or serve on, but even one instance is memorable. Why? A Board is only as strong as its weakest link. It is only as quick as its slowest member... and most Board Directors are not serving to waste their precious time. So, how does a Board ensure preparedness of all their Board Members?

  o Hold Board Members accountable to be prepared and involved both prior and during Board meetings.

  o Creation & utilization of a monthly Board Book (sometimes called a Control Book): An information package and executive-level report that typically includes performance metrics, P&L breakdown, cash statement, retention report and other pertinent information on the company. Even if formal Board meetings are happening on a quarterly basis, Boards perform at a higher level when this report package is issued monthly, potentially with a quarterly summary at the end of each quarter for study in advance of the Board Meeting. It is also useful on a monthly basis for input into the numerous Board Committee meetings that take place in-between the formal Board meetings. Efforts should be taken to keep the reporting format as consistent and repeatable as possible to allow for ease of review and familiarity.

o Management Meeting and Board Committee Meeting(s) prior to the formal Board Meeting: Let's first take a moment to clarify the highest-level responsibilities when comparing Boards and Management:

- Board Responsibility - The Board keeps the organization on track to its core values, vision, mission and strategic planning goals by:
  o Choosing the CEO (or in the case of most private companies, supporting, guiding and elevating the CEO)
  o Approving key policies and major decisions
  o Overseeing performance
  o Advocating internally and externally

- Management Responsibility – Management, via the CEO, provides the leadership to implement based on the Board's direction:
  o Developing and instituting operational policies and decisions
  o Providing transparency and performance metrics to the Board
  o Making recommendations and proposals to

the Board for decisioning

Knowing these responsibility areas, a Management meeting should be held in advance of the Board Meeting for the purpose of clarity on progress, details of any encountered challenges and understanding of any proposed changes to the strategic plan, should they be required. Similarly, it is recommended that Board Committee meetings be scheduled prior to the formal Board Meeting to ensure transparency on progress and to be prepared to highlight areas requiring the collective Board to weigh-in on. The key message here is for the detailed discussions on topics to be handled offline and outside the Board Meeting, thus leading to well-thought-out options and a recommended way forward to be proposed at the Board Meeting for collective weigh-in and vote.

Remember that all of the considerations of *'what makes a great Board'* are the individual and collective responsibility of the Board – in other words, once a Board is built, or in the process of being built, it has to be tended and cultivated. Some Boards that start out great can unravel when fundamental areas are neglected or ignored. Shortcomings then become the norm. Keep a note of the *'4 expectations of a great Board'* and the *'11 traits of a great Board'* to continuously guide the proper culture and inclusive environment of your Board.

Fact: The remarkable collapse of the energy trader, Enron Corporation, on December 1, 2001 solidified one of the largest bankruptcies ever in U.S. history. This event overlapped a time of U.S. national mourning following the terrorist attacks on 9/11 that same year. Enron galvanized a staunch legislative response in the form of the Sarbanes-Oxley Act of 2002. Sarbanes-Oxley overhauled financial reporting requirements, created a national Public Accounting Oversight Board to reform all auditing procedures, and criminalized numerous Executive and Board Director actions. An important provision of Sarbanes-Oxley was the requirement that every public Board must have an Audit Committee made up exclusively of Outside/Independent Board Directors.

Mark A. Pfister

Part II

Mark A. Pfister

5 THE ROLE OF STRATEGY

"Deciding what not to do is as important as deciding what to do."
                                                              - Steve Jobs

The effectiveness of your Board has a direct correlation to the understanding and application of strategy and governance. This is a line that will once again be mentioned in the next chapter on governance. Why mention this same sentence and concept twice in this book? Because strategy and governance play absolutely key roles in the effectiveness, efficiency and usefulness of individual Board Members and the Board as a whole. We will also further discuss the importance of strategy and governance at the individual Board Member-level in upcoming Chapter 9, *'Infusing Planes of Congruence in Your Board Model.'*

Let's first review the currently accepted definition of strategy which states, a *'strategy is a careful plan or method, usually over a period of time, to achieve a specific goal.'* What a nice and compact definition for such a complicated subject. Or so one may think. Truth is, in today's world, this definition is no longer valid. A strategy isn't always a careful plan or method, it isn't always over an implied (longer) period of time and it isn't typically to achieve just one specific goal. When we get to the end of this chapter, I would like to regroup and review with you what I believe is the current-day definition of strategy, taking into consideration many influential inputs and trends - I think you may be surprised by what strategy has become in light of Artificial Intelligence (AI), Big Data and other societal trending.

The History of Strategy

Whenever I get the chance, especially when on my speaking tours, I try to spend quality time, albeit brief, on the history of strategy – where it came from, how it has been applied, how it has evolved and of course, try to predict where it is going. In my world, strategy is inextricably linked to leadership. I don't believe an innovative strategy can exist without strong leadership and I don't believe strong leadership can exist without an innovative strategy. There are not many writings or educational forums that make this somewhat obvious link, but when it comes to Boards, it is imperative.

All throughout history, we hear and read of instances of amazing strategies being conceived and implemented. In 70BC the Roman Poet Virgil tells the story of the Trojan horse when Greek forces entered Troy's heavily guarded city gates. In 1532, Machiavelli's book entitled 'The Prince' offers clever success 'recipes' for government officials and remains a must-read for politicians and political science majors to this day. In 1993, the book 'Reengineering The Corporation' by Michael Hammer and James Champy revolutionizes ideas of corporate structure by including processes, organization and culture considerations into the mix. The list of notable strategies is endless, but they do have common threads. Can you guess what the common threads are?

There are three, to be exact. Over the course of approximately

2,500 years of documented strategy, there are arguably only three professions which have benefitted from the use of strategy:

- o Warmongers: Strategies applied to avoiding wars and winning wars
- o Politicians: Strategies applied to gaining power and holding power
- o Business Leaders: Strategies applied to building power and creating monopolies

In my early days of studying strategy, it was fascinating to see that with all of the so-called strategies that were concocted and implemented across human history, all of them could actually be neatly housed within the 3 *professions* of war, politics and business. It is not by chance that many business strategies and competition for market traction are likened to war and politics... but we shouldn't be surprised – business and political strategies were adopted and adapted from war strategies! And vice-versa.

The evolution of strategy across these three professions is equally as interesting.[15]

- o From 500BC through 1900, there are two major strategy evolution phases that took place. The first is *war strategies and conflict deterrence.* The second is *politics and exclusivity.*
  - – War Strategies and Conflict Deterrence: In 500BC, Sun Tzu, a Chinese general, military strategist and philosopher practiced and wrote about military strategies. His book, *'The Art of War,'* is the first known detailed strategy documentation ever created. Amazingly, many of these strategies have been used in modern times. Concepts such as *'avoiding war was just as important as winning a war'*

as well as *'winning a battle without fighting is the best way to win'* are just two of many profound concepts and quotes from Sun Tzu. His book has been translated to most languages and is worth the time to read.

- Politics and Exclusivity: When it comes to the *'politics'* channel, Niccolò Machiavelli epitomizes this phase of strategy evolution. He was an Italian Renaissance historian, politician, diplomat, philosopher, humanist and writer. His book, *'The Prince,'* is still a valid handbook for politicians. Due to some of the book's devious suggestions, the word *'Machiavellian'* has come to refer to acts of deceit and manipulation. When it comes to the *'exclusivity'* side, John D. Rockefeller epitomizes this phase of strategy evolution. Business strategy through the 1800s focused on the exclusive control or supply of trade in commodities or services. John D. Rockefeller applied exclusivity strategies to monopolize the oil trade business under the premise that if you control everything, there is no competition. This strategy worked quite well for him – to this day he still holds the top seat as the richest person in modern times with an inflation-corrected net worth of $340 billion. Astounding.

○ From 1900 through 1968, the strategy evolution phase is classified as *'Industrial Proficiency.'* By 1904, the monopolistic practices of the *'top few'* were under attack following muckraker Ida Tarbell's 1904 expose on John D. Rockefeller when she published *'The History of the Standard Oil Company.'* This early instance of investigative journalism initiated a wave of government involvement in breaking up monopolies – and forced the need for concurrent strategy shifts. John D. Rockefeller adapted quickly. His *'open book'* approach of willingly showing his numbers and ability to sell oil products at a profit for prices well below competitors' production costs forced competitors to sell their operations or risk folding. This *'price war'* strategy approach prevailed until 1968 with Peter Drucker, known as the *'Father of Modern Management'* summarizing almost all strategies employed within this phase as only a *'competition on price.'*

o   1969 through the 1990s is known as the *'Strategy Heydays.'* Michael Porter, the author of *'What is Strategy,'* summarizes this phase as containing two major components: a) *"do what everyone else is doing , but spend less money doing it"* (somewhat of a leftover from the previous Industrial Proficiency phase) and b) *"do something no one else can do."* The previous evolutionary phase's *'competition on price'*-only strategy had major shortcomings as it has the propensity to drive all companies in the industry to the lowest common denominator, in both cost and selling price. This eventually and inevitably leads shrinking profits to miniscule amounts to even stay in the game. A great example of this diminishing return side-effect was painfully witnessed in the airline industry in the 1980s – an industry that did not adapt to newer, more successful strategies. Following deregulation in 1978, the airline industry kept aligned with *'Industrial Proficiency'* strategies where fierce ticket price wars spiraled the entire industry into low/no profit territory, thus ultimately leading to large-scale bankruptcies. Price competition alone, as it was proven, was not the only consideration for successful business strategy. But when the other strategic consideration of *'do something no one else can do'* is introduced to run in parallel with a low-cost strategy, this was revolutionary. Cost competitiveness no longer meant that you had to be the cheapest, just as long as you additionally offered something of great value to offset a slightly increased cost. This combination had the positive effect of opening many new markets as industries expanded with technology innovations, advancements, and offerings.

o The 1990s through the 2010s are known as the '*Strategic Proliferation*' phase of strategy. This strategy phase shows a combination and joining of 3 concepts: a) build on what you already do, b) do something new and c) react opportunistically to emerging possibilities. This proved to be a very balanced approach in theory – all three of these areas seemed achievable. Unfortunately, as the phase is titled, I have grown to be weary of the word '*proliferation*,' as it typically is not used with positive connotation. This is a shame due to the fact that the word implies availability and abundance. It is ultimately what we do with that availability and abundance that can sway the word to the positive or negative side. My weariness is warranted in this instance. Know that it wasn't the actual strategy theory that caused trouble in this phase, it truly was the proliferation of countless sub-strategies that caused the issues. The proliferation of sub-strategies, made possible by the internet, caused difficulty for many companies when attempting to choose the right one. Companies that did their homework and right-sized their strategy methodology did well. However, if they settled and hastily made a decision, their chances of kicking-off a strategy, or strategic process that did not directly fit their business, or industry was high. And, as the available strategies multiplied, so did the complexity. This period of strategy evolution rendered many companies in a paralysis state and led to billions of dollars in failed initiatives. There existed other headwinds, also. Michael E. Raynor, author of '*The Strategy Paradox*,' revealed a fascinating collision between commitment and uncertainty that reared its head during this timeframe. Phrased in a question, *"how does a leader make choices based on assumptions about a future they cannot predict?"* A paradox indeed, but not something that hasn't been encountered before. The only difference now is likely the accelerating speed at which the unpredictable future is heading towards you.

o The current evolution of strategy of the 2010s (or post-2010s) actually doesn't have a globally-accepted phase-name currently. Even so, I have begun to call our current strategic phase *'Amorphic Strategy'* in my speaking engagements. It just seems to be such a fitting name based on all of the new and moving parts within modern day successful strategies - the fluidity and shape-changing properties that force strategists, Boards, and leaders to weigh against seemingly multiplying data and risk/reward inputs.

Strategy of today is unequivocally different than in the past. Why? Because the application of strategy is now applied to everything from the most mundane single task to the most highly complex, multi-year program. Strategy is no longer applicable to only those areas that have a defined budget, scope, and timeline associated with them. Strategy has become commoditized through advancements in disruptive technology, and most importantly, progress in Artificial Intelligence, big data, and machine learning. The ability to simultaneously (and continuously) build a strategy and *'grade'* its likelihood of success, as well as risk of failure prior to implementation is no longer science fiction.

Add geopolitical influences and generational motivations into the equation and the need to adapt a strategy more quickly to change becomes paramount. All of these inputs add to the concept of *'simultaneity,'* the relationships between multiple events happening at the same time, and deserves a strategy within itself.

The point of this history and evolution lesson on strategy is to illustrate the current speed of change and accelerating knowledge-base in this area. Boards, and more specifically, individual Board Members, are limited in their effectiveness when they lack an in-depth understanding of strategy, where it came from, and where it is headed.

Figure 10a: The Board's Proposed Role in Strategy - Practical View[15a]

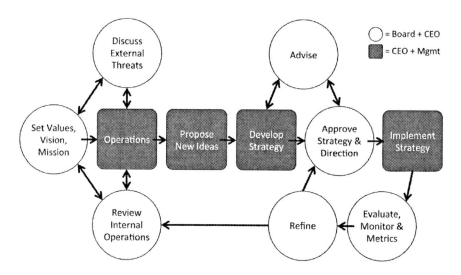

Boards have become much more involved with strategy creation for the companies they serve, an area that has historically been the sole (or major) responsibility of the CEO. The driving forces behind this trend include the understanding of how complex markets have become and the fear that a strategy created (or guided) and endorsed by a single individual (CEO) has exponential risk.

Additionally, the old-school concept of a Board approving their CEO's multi-year strategy and simply graduating to a governance mode for 2 - 5 years is no longer valid. That speed of change dilemma again. A successful Board strategy needs to include a quarterly review and evaluation of the company's current strategy. Is the company strategy still valid? Are there new industry or competitor trends that need to be considered? Are there new technologies in their infancy stages that could have a future positive or detrimental impact on the company, or its offerings? Where can the data metrics to vet and support current and in-play strategic decisions be acquired and reviewed? What areas, if any, should be considered for a course-correction, or tweak? These important considerations and thought-processes cannot be accomplished with Board Members who do not fully understand the foundational elements of strategy and its proper application.

Reported in the 2016–2017 'NACD *Public Company Governance Survey,'*[15d] one of the findings highlights an interesting challenge to Board engagement regarding strategy-setting. Due to intense, short-term performance pressure placed on Boards, as well as management, 75% of respondents reported that management's focus on long-term value creation has been compromised by pressure to deliver short-term results. 29% reported that pressure on Boards to focus on short-term performance inhibits their ability to effectively oversee long-term strategy development and governance. These challenges in the public sector will most likely continue to varying degrees, but a mindful Board knows that it is possible to create, oversee, and govern a strategy that satisfies both the typically shorter-term investor desires, while simultaneously adapting to a longer-term strategic view.

Additionally found in this 2016-2017 NACD study,[15d] more than half of the Boards claimed that active involvement in the development of strategy was a goal for major improvement over the following 12 month period. This is a positive trend, indeed.

The Board's collective recognition that involvement in strategy creation, along with the previously-accepted strategy oversight and governance, has an exponentially positive effect on the overall organization and is a powerful awakening for Boards. A Board's deeper, first-hand knowledge of the all-important strategy allows for greater understanding, discussion, and deliberation when addressing this topic. An added benefit is the Board's shared strategic accountability and ownership together with the CEO, preventing *'sides'* from forming when needed adjustments or changes are required in the strategic plan.

Figure 10b: The Board's Proposed Role in Strategy – Potential Board Additional *'Controlled'* Involvement[15a]

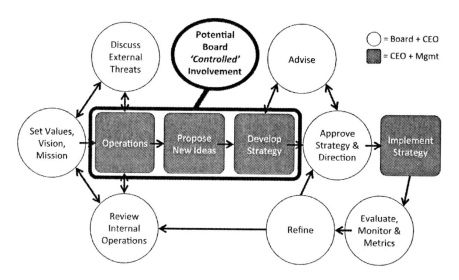

Now that you have a far-reaching knowledge of formal strategy, let's revisit and redefine the definition of strategy as it applies to modern Board application:

Old Definition: *'Strategy is a careful plan or method, usually over a period of time, to achieve a specific goal'*

New Definition: *'Strategy is a set of guiding principles that, when communicated and adopted, generates a desired pattern of integrated decision making'*

It should be noted that what previously was the definition of Board strategy, which contained hard, tangible deliverables and specific outcomes, is now more of a concept and process including *'desired behaviors.'* It is the Board's role to foster an environment which *'generates a desired pattern of integrated decision making,'* for both the Board, as well as the overall organization. This is fully in support of a more fluid and accommodating approach to continuously guiding a strategy on an ongoing basis – hence, an *'amorphic strategy.'*

Where possible, I prefer to give examples of relevant strategy-in-action to help with the understanding of its absolute prevalence and power. My article, *'How Big Data Wrecked Democracy Forever: A Pivot in Campaigning Strategy That Changed The World,'*[15b] published in May of 2017, shows how strategy was applied in a global sense with far-reaching consequences. I would like to share it with you now.

You may initially be thinking I've finally been lured into the political fray and now writing about politics with polarizing consequences. You would be wrong. That's not my style. I will even confidently claim that after you read this example, you still won't be able to tell my political affiliations, as that is not the purpose of this example. The purpose is to show how a change in strategy, and an acceptance of change, can make all of the difference - especially when it comes to the political realm. Ok, now that we have gotten my disclaimers out of the way, let's get to the example by first asking a provocative question:

Are you aware of how the strategic voter-targeting mechanics of the 2016 U.S. election differed from the 2008 U.S. election?

Let me give you a *'big'* hint: Big Data vs. Social Media

Taking all of the noise, presidential candidate preferences and political party affiliations out of the equation, there was actually a quiet and massive movement happening under our feet (and in our online news feeds) leading up to the U.S. November 2016 presidential election day - and we didn't even notice...

First, a quick primer. If we look back at the 2008 U.S. presidential election, a major component of a successful candidate's voter canvassing approach included a large social media strategy. Some might claim the social media strategy was the heaviest component in 2008. Reach a large voter audience with a focused common thread of social alignment through popular technology. Period. This was a mechanism that reached a significant number of people within social media *'groups.'* The important word here being *'groups,'* not individuals, which at the time was a cutting-edge way to reach targeted demographics and cater your message directly to larger sets of people. It served as the outlet, or *'ends,'* to reach large, affiliated audiences. It worked. And it worked amazingly well. That was then.

Big Data: Extremely large data sets that may be analyzed computationally to reveal patterns, trends, and associations, especially relating to human behavior and interactions.

Fast forward to the 2016 U.S. presidential election. Totally different ballgame. Strategy evolution at play again. Yes, social media remained a component of voter-gaining strategies. However, instead of social media, now combined with other big data sources, only being deployed for the *'ends'* of reaching voters, it pivoted to become the *'means.'* In other words, it was the data gleaned from our online activities (social media, credit card purchases, affiliations, etc.) that allowed for a massive data *'pool'* that no longer only targeted large social groups, it now could be analyzed and targeted to you *personally*. By name. By skin color. By political affiliation. By sex. Even by sexual orientation. And this process was amazingly accurate. Every additional '*data-generating*' day that goes by allows analytics tools to predict '*you*' with even more accuracy. When it came to political articles in your news feeds leading up to the 2016 U.S. presidential election, it was not by chance. You were targeted and force-fed items that you both wanted to hear and did not want to hear. These articles were positioned in a chronological order of agreement / disagreement, for you personally, that has proven in studies to sway feelings and beliefs... including how you would vote - which for most people this decision is based on feeling. Here is some background on how it happened:

2008: Research performed by Michal Kosinski and David Stillwell, fellow PhD students at Cambridge University, developed an extremely accurate mechanism and process to analyze individuals (potential voters) in minute detail solely based on their Facebook activity.

2009 and Onward: Credit card purchasing data, which has historically been sold as anonymous and aggregated data, as well as other large information data sets, becomes more readily available for purchase - with further personal identifying details included. Trending, metrics and analytics of this data becomes more of a commodity.

2013: The company Cambridge Analytica forms, providing data mining and data analytics for strategic communication in electoral processes.

2014: Cambridge Analytica is involved in 44 U.S. political races, and also worked on behalf of the pro-Brexit campaign in the U.K., which many believe served as the proving grounds for large-scale political implementations.

2016: Cambridge Analytica engaged in U.S. presidential election by the Republican National Committee. Democratic National Committee decides not to utilize this canvassing strategy.

2016's U.S. presidential election had two very different candidates, so the line between their beliefs and approaches was very well defined. Big Data was still deployed and many behind-the-scenes strategists believe that it was the differentiator in the RNC winning the election (they do not believe it was Comey, or Russia, or Twitter, etc.)... And what about two candidates in the future where they are both closer to center and somewhat less polarizing. Will Big Data be able to more easily sway the voter mentality (and buyer mentality, for that matter) one way through a targeted campaign? I believe the answer is a resounding "*yes.*"

As you now know, previous history going back to 500 BC has shown that the evolution of strategy followed the '*profession*' path of war, politics and then business, with business being the most recent catalyst to further strategy concepts and approaches. I believe political strategy may have quietly overtaken business strategy for the top seat in strategy evolution once again - and we didn't even notice.

So, why do I believe that Big Data wrecked democracy forever? It is not due to the outcome of the U.S. election, or the leveraging of technology, or the ever-evolving role of data in our society. I believe in Big Data. I use it as a fundamental input in my strategy creation and also as a way for Boards to validate existing strategies. But when it is used in such a way to '*condition*' us to behave, react, vote, etc. in a predisposed way, that is likely crossing the line. It can use our openness and free way of life against us. It can become a leverage point to turn our own lifestyles against us. Scary thought, but it is already a reality.

...But what a strategy it was and will continue to be, no arguing that. Effective, efficient and able to target individuals on a massive scale, proving once again that the proper strategy always wins. I guess we can't have it both ways.

The point of sharing this story is to illustrate how strategy surrounds us every day. It is ever-present and ever-evolving. It is powerful. For leaders and Board Directors, it needs to be fully understood.

Key Takeaway: Every Board Member must have a fundamental understanding of strategy, and where it is heading, to truly be effective and viable to the companies they serve. For Board candidates, probe for their level of understanding and proficiency in this area. For existing Board Members, leverage continuing education opportunities to raise proficiency levels.

Board Strategy Fact: On the topic of Artificial Intelligence (A.I.), a Hong Kong VC fund named Deep Knowledge Ventures appointed an algorithm to its Board in 2014. Yes, an algorithm is a listed and seated Board Member in this company and gets a vote on all investment opportunities. VITAL, this *"Board Member's"* name, is the sixth member of Deep Knowledge Venture's Board. Although not exactly A.I. at this point, that is the long-term goal of the seat...[15c]

Mark A. Pfister

6 THE ROLE OF GOVERNANCE

"The speed of decision-making is the essence of good governance."
                                                        - Piyush Goyal

The effectiveness of your Board has a direct correlation to the understanding and application of strategy and governance. Hopefully you remember this was the same introduction sentence in the previous chapter. I mentioned that I would repeat this line due to strategy and governance playing absolutely critical roles in the effectiveness, efficiency, and usefulness of individual Board Members, and the Board as a whole.

Governance Definition: *'Governance is the unification of policies, systems, and structures that aligns leadership to take effective action with accountability.'*

The term *'governance'* has an interesting history with its believed first appearance in 370 BC by Plato. It is derived from the Greek word kubernáo, meaning *'to steer,'* – quite fitting when it is applied in the modern Board space. In the 16th, 17th and 18th centuries, the term was mainly applied to ruling a country, as in

England's numerous *'governance of the realm'* references in historic documents. This leads to the modern day word association with its adoption in a broader business sense in the 1990s by economists and political scientists when addressing merger and acquisition activity in the United States.[16] Today, the term governance is ubiquitous in the Board space and has likely become a parallel word where Boards are referenced.

Fig 10c: Governance History[17]

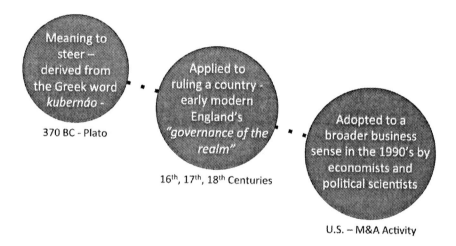

So, why do we need governance? How does governance elevate companies? Let's first agree that business complexity is continuously increasing and an ever-changing economic and political climate is accelerating. These challenges place elevated demands on companies that must be quickly and systematically addressed to stay relevant. Governance, as the earlier definition proclaims, should truly be a framework and process that aligns leadership to take effective action with accountability in the areas of company policies, systems and structures.

Figure 11: Governance Framework[17]

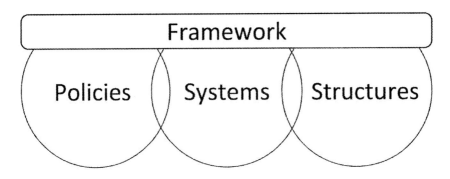

When it comes to governance, primary considerations are placed on how these three important areas interface and integrate with one another. This key framework mechanism is a crucial one when applied to the responsibilities and accountability of the Board. In its simplest state, this *process* is essentially what a Board is *governing* for the company it is serving. In my experience, this simple concept remains elusive for so many Boards due to tactical task distractions, meandering agendas and poor leadership. Additionally, a common question remains for many Boards – is governance the responsibility of the entire Board or individual Board members? I believe the correct answer to be *'both,'* as each individual Board Member should constantly be on guard to keep the entire Board within its governance guardrails. This fundamental learning is mentioned, as this important chapter reminds us, that without each individual Board Member's fundamental understanding of governance, it is simply impossible to keep an entire Board on track to its governance mandate.

Now, let's expand on our framework in further detail to offer clarification on the delineation between the Board's governance responsibilities and management's corporate governance responsibilities.

Figure 12: Board Governance Framework[18]

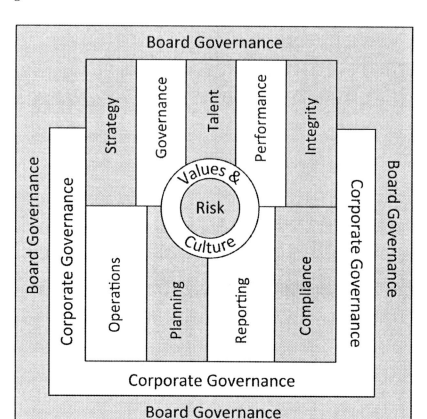

Notice the direct interaction of the Board in the areas of strategy, governance, talent, performance, and integrity. Strategy, as mentioned in the previous chapter, has historically been viewed as the sole responsibility of the CEO, however, this is no longer the case. As you now know, the Board should have shared responsibility and accountability in this area.

In the center of this governance model, it should not be surprising that 'risk' holds the coveted bullseye position. I like to add 'overseeing uncertainty' as an additional viewpoint. Maneuvering through risk, both real and implied, is obviously the purpose of all governance actions. It is surprising to many, however, that 'values

& culture' holds an equally important center position when discussing governance. This is because sound (and *'lived'*) company values lead to a meaningful and grounded culture that ultimately lowers organization risk.

Values = Culture = Lower Organization Risk

This is a profound point and should always be central to individual Board Members, and the entire Board, in all dealings, encounters and interactions with the companies they serve.

Let's further walk through this *'values'* concept by referencing certain current events. With all of the recent high-profile media attention on sexual harassment in the workplace, the main word that continuously resonates is *'values.'* How can these trust-breaking and reputation-jarring instances continually happen in a company? How is it that a single person, or group, can behave like this for so long, decades in some cases, without appropriate repercussions? The answer is a lack of values, at both the individual and company level.

In my speaking engagements around the country on various Board topics, I have continued to emphasize the importance of values at the Board level, including how a company's values sit above its vision and mission.[17] Why? Because company values are guiding principles that dictate behavior and action of employees, team members and even vendors. These guiding principles define the foundation for governance.

Additionally, a company's values should be *'owned'* at the Board level. This statement has garnered an uptick in audience questions regarding the topic - something I am always happy to explain and can be visualized in the following diagram:

Figure 13: Values-Positioned Governance

A company that knows what it stands for in terms of ethics, principles, and beliefs is an organization that is light-years ahead of competitors lacking this vital realization.

Values-Positioned Governance Example

My go-to example when speaking about values and their inextricable link to governance starts with Roy E. Disney and his quote that will live forever:

> *"It's not hard to make decisions when*
> *you know what your values are."*

Roy E. Disney was a longtime senior executive, Board Member, and Director Emeritus for The Walt Disney Company, which was founded by his father, Roy O. Disney and uncle, Walt Disney. Roy E. believed that every company decision could be made quickly and effectively simply by referencing the company's values. He was a master in effectively implementing this *'Values Decisioning'* governance methodology and his story is worth telling.

Roy E. Disney was born in Los Angeles in 1930 and watched as his father and uncle continued to build and grow The Walt Disney Company. This modern powerhouse was founded in 1923 as the Disney Brothers Cartoon Studio, establishing itself as a leader in the animation industry and later expanding into live film production, television, and theme parks. Roy E. graduated from Pomona College in 1951 and subsequently became an assistant director and producer at Disney. In 1967, he was elected to the company's Board of Directors.

It is what happened in the upcoming years where Roy E.'s commitment to his company's and his own core values that truly makes him exceptional. In 1977, Roy E. resigned as an executive from Disney over disagreements with corporate decisions. He felt the company had lost itself and created a stifling environment that limited creative pursuits... and company numbers reflected this. He did retain his Board seat, however, until 1984 when he resigned during a corporate takeover battle. This is when his first 'Save Disney' campaign started in an effort to stave off a hostile takeover of Disney with the goal of dismantling the company and selling off its assets. In defiance, Roy E. led a group of investors which successfully halted the hostile takeover. Yes, you guessed it - his approach was to bring the company back on track to its original values... and it succeeded in rallying big money to the rescue.

Disney's Values are committed to:

- Continued **innovation** and technology,
- Striving for **high standards of excellence,**
- **Positive, inclusive ideas about family,** which provide enjoyment for all ages,
- Continuing a tradition of **timeless storytelling** that

delights and inspires, and

- To **honor and respect decency** in order to inspire trust in the company.

Roy E. would be tested again in the second *'Save Disney'* campaign he started in 2003. He cited *"serious differences of opinion about the direction and style of management"* in the company with Michael Eisner at the helm. Similar to the first *'Save Disney'* campaign, albeit this time with a rallied existing shareholder base, Roy E. was once again able to prevail by aligning his campaign to the foundational values of the company.

Throughout all of the struggles, hardships and uphill battles that Roy E. fought over the years to save the company founded by his father and uncle, he always credited his quick decision-making and success in seemingly overwhelming circumstances to his steadfast belief in the company's values, as well as his own values. Once again, he knew the secret that *"it's not hard to make decisions when you know what your values are."*

Roy E. was the last member of the Disney family to be actively involved in the company. He died in 2009, but his relentless pursuit of The Disney Company's values-guided decision-making lives on to this day. Truly a worthy governance legacy to bequeath upon the company he loved so much.

Give it a try in the future! Pick a day in which you will attempt to make all decisions that cross your desk simply by referencing your company's values. Don't take more than 10 seconds to make each decision. Then, compare this to the actual outcome after all appropriate channels are consulted. You are going to be surprised.

Another legacy that can be partially attributed to Roy E. Disney through his pursuit of showcasing values at the Board level is equally reflective. Many Board Members, Board candidates, as well as executive search/placement companies, adopted the importance of first ensuring alignment of the company's values with those of the Board Member/candidate before anything else. After all, misalignment of values will lead to a fractured culture and ineffective governance. It makes sense that a check for values alignment should take place at the onset as this will save much time and effort when evaluating Board candidates.

Furthermore to the topic of governance, it is important to understand the formal structures of multiple governance models when building, operating within, or evaluating Boards. A common oversight for Boards and Board Directors is that they either don't know what model they are operating in, or they don't know that there are multiple models. Both scenarios are dangerous predicaments as they increase the risk of misaligned interaction styles and increased decisioning time.

Figure 14: Traditional Governance Model[19]

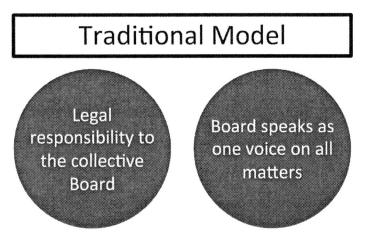

The Traditional Governance Model is the oldest model for corporate governance, but is somewhat outdated by today's standards. It assigns the legal responsibility to the collective Board and the Board speaks as one voice on all matters.

Figure 15: Carver Governance Model[19]

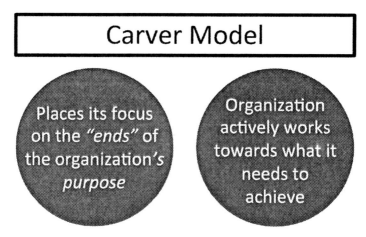

The Carver Governance Model is typically instituted in nonprofit and for-profit organizations. The Board gives the CEO the bulk of the responsibility, within defined and acceptable limits, for using the means to get to the ends. In parallel, the organization actively works towards it's overall goals and what it needs to achieve.

Figure 16: Cortex Governance Model[19]

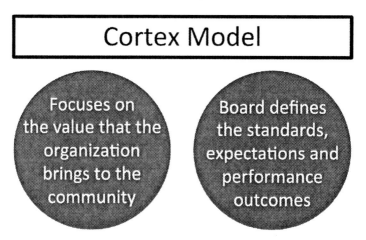

The Cortex Governance Model focuses on the value that the organization brings to the community. Clarifying and setting outcomes to achieve success become the primary duty of the

Board under this model.

Figure 17: Consensus Governance Model[19]

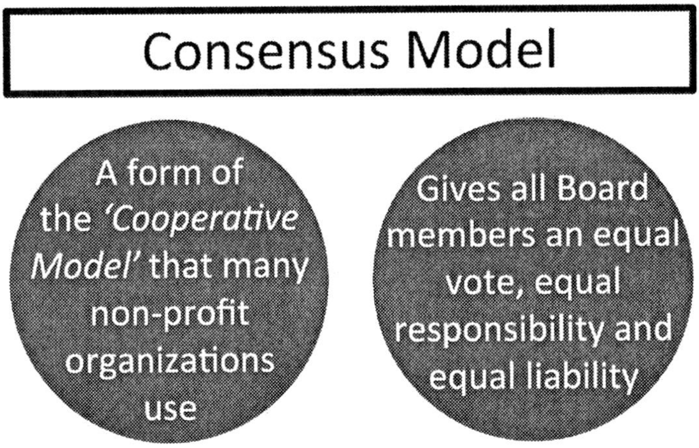

Consensus Model

A form of the *'Cooperative Model'* that many non-profit organizations use

Gives all Board members an equal vote, equal responsibility and equal liability

The Consensus Governance Model, sometimes called the *'process model,'* is typically appropriate for companies without major shareholders. It's a form of a *'cooperative model'* that many nonprofit organizations use and gives all Board Members an equal vote, equal responsibility, and equal liability.

Figure 18: Competency Governance Model[19]

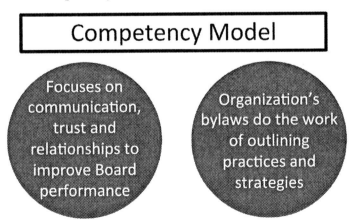

Competency Model

Focuses on communication, trust and relationships to improve Board performance

Organization's bylaws do the work of outlining practices and strategies

A company Board with interest in developing knowledge and

skills of Board Members will typically lean towards the Competency Governance Model. It focuses on trust, relationships, and communication to improve performance of the Board and its Board Members. Practices and strategies of this model are typically outlined in detail in the company's bylaws.

In many cases, one stand-alone governance model is not sufficient to satisfy the needs of all organizations. In these instances, it is common for boards to combine attributes of multiple governance models in an effort to satisfy the requirements of the Board and the company. This approach can be quite effective, but caution must be taken to avoid combining conflicting governance approaches, or principles that can lead to confusion and misalignment. An example of a mixed model that I frequently implement is seen in the following figure and has the benefit of leveraging *best in class* practices from multiple proven governance methodologies. When you understand the inner components of each corporate governance model, it becomes easier to combine the attributes that will most benefit your Board and organization.

Figure 19: Mixed Governance Model (Example)

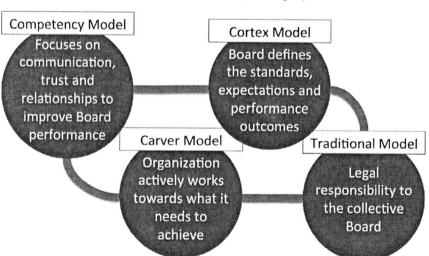

All governance models may have components that can be evaluated for a *'mixed'* approach, custom designed for your organization and Board.

There exists another major consideration for Boards and Board Members to fully understand when referencing and applying governance. I felt compelled to get a little more tactical for this next section due to the profound effect it has had in aligning and harmonizing governance efforts for Boards. For the first time in history, leaders and employees from five generations are interacting daily in the workplace and on Boards. This is an incredible concept to imagine. If you estimate that each *'defined generation'* is considered to occupy a span of roughly 20 years, the life experiences and working-style differences across multiple generations are immense. Even more incredible is how technology advances in recent decades have accelerated the change in workplace communication and interaction norms - which some argue has further defined the delineation between generations.

So, what's the issue? Its more of a challenge than an issue, as I see it, and it needs to be addressed by every company, leader, and Board to remain effective and competitive: *"How do you successfully create a governance model in an environment with so many varying motivation, communication, and work-style needs?"* This is not an easy responsibility to overcome, but the following simple steps have been quite effective for companies I advise, and for the Boards I serve.

Step 1: Analyze. Do you know your company and Board well? Possibly, but it is likely that you have not spent time analyzing the generational makeup of your Board Members or company leaders. This is very important and foundational information to know in order to initiate the process of harmonizing all of these generations into a cohesive, efficient, and productive group. To match an appropriate governance model to reach the optimal resonance within your Board at the macro level, you must first understand what generations make up your Board and the company's leadership (and potentially the organization's entire workforce). I suggest creating a special project to gather this information and view the numbers as well as the percentages. Remember that this concept can also be applied at the management level or a micro-level to projects, programs, lines of business, etc. to maximize company understanding.

Goal of Step 1: Listing and breakdown percentages of your Board and organization's generational makeup.

Step 2: Research. People of each generation share an '*age position*' in time. This inevitably includes social trends and other historical-defining events encountered while inhabiting the same phase of life. For example, Generation X, who came of age during the Information Age, was influenced and shaped much differently than their Baby Boomer parents who came of age during a time of values experimentation and challenging of authority. These unique experiences create common beliefs, behaviors, and values that can be attributed to a specific generation. This has a profound effect on not only the understanding of governance, but also how it is applied. I recommend that even if you document less than 5 generations in your evaluation group, it is worthwhile to research all 5 due to the inherent benefits and understanding it brings.

I have found the following 2 charts to be very informational and a great starting point for research and categorization when evaluating and building Boards:

Figure 20: Perceived Generational Traits – Members of each generation that *'best'* display the following characteristics[20]

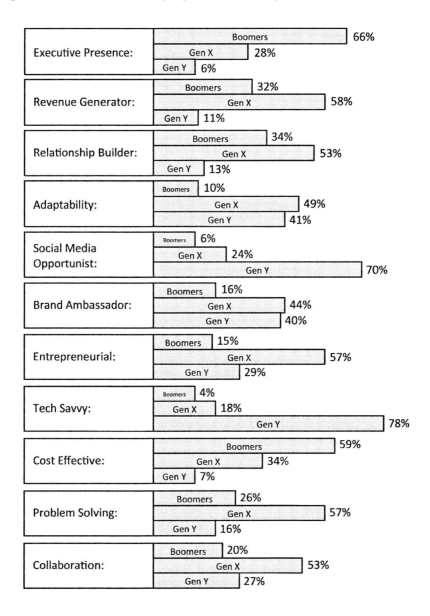

Figure 21: Generational Categories

Century	Generation	Sub-Generation	Born	Notable Occurrences
20th	Greatest Generation	G.I. Generation	1901-1924	Experienced WWII in adulthood
		Silent Generation	1925-1945	Experienced and fought in WWII / Civil Rights Movement
	Baby Boomers	Boom Generation / Hippie	1946-1964	Space exploration, first modern 'counterculture'
	Generation X	Baby Busters	1965-1980	Experienced Vietnam War / Cold War
		MTV Generation / Boomerang Generation	1975-1985	Rise of mass media / end of the Cold War
	Generation Y	Echo Boom / Generation McGuire	1978-1990	Rise of the Information Age / Internet / War on Terror / Iraq War / Rising commodity prices
21st	Generation Z	New Silent Generation	1995-2007	Rise of the Information Age / Internet / Dot Com Bubble / Digital Globalization

Goal of Step 2: Answer the question, '*what do the members of each generation value, how does this apply to the Board, and what governance model(s) are appropriate?*'

Step 3: Understand and Apply. You now have a view of the generations within your Board (step 1) and an understanding of the values and motivations for each of these generations (step 2). Just as each of us have our good and bad traits, so do the generations. I would argue that it is not about good or bad, strengths or weaknesses, but rather the *differences* and leading through them. Said differently, know what makes each generation tick to make the most of the differences. Some initial questions you may want to ask yourself with your new-found data as you continue your process include:

- Do fellow Board Members communicate in such a way that reaches all of the generations within the Board? Each generation responds differently to each type of communication medium and even when, where and how each generation consumes content varies. A good article as a starting point on syncing communication to ensure alignment within your Board environment is *'Championing a Multi-Generational Workforce With Visual Communication'* by Matt Pierce.[21]

- Does your Board have an acknowledgement mechanism (a *'rewards and recognition program'* of sorts) that leverages the motivational chords across each generation? A multi-faceted acknowledgement approach typically works best.

- Does the physical Board meeting and workforce environment cater towards all generations? Does it look towards the future? For many companies, the *'Age of the Cubicle'* is quickly drawing to a close, and there may be value in designing multiple work environments within the same office space to accommodate generational workspace preferences. Office furniture companies such as Knoll have taken notice of the generational needs and published the whitepaper, *Generational Preferences: A Glimpse Into the Future Office*[22] - worth a read.

- Is the Board aware of each generation's optimal work conditions and has it created policies that foster flexibility and productivity? This typically applies to meetings and work associated with the Board Committees, but it is an important overall consideration in the Board's internal governance model.

- Does the Board understand each generation's learning and teaching styles? Many companies have spent unbelievable amounts of effort and money on training programs that are outdated and do not *'reach'* their intended audience. Worse yet, they are either targeted towards one generation's style or have attempted to incorporate pieces of each generation's styles, rendering the entire program ineffective. A great reference on learning and teaching styles by generation can be researched within the presentation, '*Effective Employee Training in a Multi-Generational Workforce.*'[23]

Goal of Step 3: Create your Generational Strategic Implementation Plan

Know that this generational exercise may be the most important thing you as a Board Member do within the companies you serve in the upcoming year. This process may even help clarify previous conflicts within an existing Board and prevent them in the future. Boards that do not work well together achieve very little. This is not only terrible for a company, but can also tarnish a Board Member's, or entire Board's, reputation.

The point of this more tactical generational overview is to point out that there are numerous undercurrents within every Board due to generational conditioning and partialities. Knowing, addressing, and incorporating them into your Board design and ongoing governance is imperative.

Key Takeaway: Every Board Member must have a fundamental understanding of governance and its multiple models to truly be effective and viable to the companies they serve. An exercise that reviews multiple governance models alongside an assessment of a Board's governance responsibilities is a worthwhile exercise. All governance models may have components that can be evaluated for a '*mixed*' approach and custom design for your company. Generational predispositions also play a major role in deciding the appropriate governance model and communication approaches to ensure effectiveness. For Board candidates, probe for their level of understanding and proficiency in this area. For existing Board Members, leverage continuing education opportunities to raise proficiency levels.

Governance Fact: A study conducted in 2000 comparing the returns, after the cost of capital, for dozens of companies rated A+ in corporate governance concluded there was *"no quantitative evidence to either prove or disprove a link between solely corporate governance and performance,"* at least as indicated by externally observable measures. Similar studies conducted in the U.K., Southeast Asia, and elsewhere have generated similarly conflicting findings – proof that governance alone is not the entire formula for a Board's success.[23a]

Mark A. Pfister

7 EVALUATING VALUES, VISION, & MISSION

"Vision is a destination – a fixed point to which we focus all effort. Strategy is a route – an adaptable path to get us where we want to go."

- Simon Sinek

Expanding upon the previous chapter's principles on a company's values being inextricably linked to governance, let's take a moment to further analyze values, as well as vision and mission, and their interesting tie-in to the Board space.

First, it is important to understand the true meaning and importance of values, vision and mission for your company:

Values: Guiding principles that dictate behavior and action of your Board, employees, team members, and even your vendors. Are Board Members in your company results-focused? Do they communicate effectively and efficiently? You likely have an ideal Board Member predisposition that exemplifies your company and resonates with your constituents. Have you built an environment that fosters who you and your Board strive to be? Company values examples include:

- Collaboration: *'We obtain the perspective of others and share our own to achieve outstanding results.'*

- Feedback & Development: *'We ask for and provide appropriate and constructive feedback to further develop ourselves and others.'*

Vision: Outlines what a company wants to be, or enable, in the future. Have you created the vision of your successful Point of Arrival (POA) for the company and the Board? Does everyone on the Board and in the company know where they are headed and why it is important? A simple example of an effective Vision statement for a technology company can be:

'A country where every citizen has unencumbered internet access.'

Mission: Describes what a company does well now. Is your mission something that everyone in your company and the Board feels compelled to rally behind? Does it clearly state what your current business actions and daily corporate life support? A clear mission statement example, again for the same example technology company, can be:

"Our company's mission is to provide affordable and readily-available internet solutions to underprivileged communities improving their quality of life"

So, what does all of this have to do with building an effective Board?

I have found that effective and viable Board Members are attracted to companies with meaningful values, a strong vision statement and a resonating mission.[24] And once a candidate is in place on the Board, these same Board Members become the guides and governance leaders of these three important facets of all companies. It is very easy for new clients and offerings, a large contract or even a slow revenue quarter to divert a company from its foundational values, vision, and mission underpinnings - an effective Board allows for the important parallel paths of effective operations and strategic focus in these 3 areas to thrive, regardless of outside potentially diverting forces.

In scenarios where you are searching for exceptional Board candidates, leverage your company's values, vision, and mission to attract your ideal applicants. Create a *'Board Pitch Book'* (a pitch deck of sorts) that includes, among other details:

- An outline of the core values of the organization and illustrate how these values guide the Board's actions and decision-making.

- The company's vision statement and why it is an imperative and worthwhile endeavor for Board Members, executives and employees to support.

- The company's mission statement with examples of how the organization, inclusive of the Board, is supportive and steadfast in its sponsorship of it.

- Additional: The company's employee Credo. Credo comes straight from the Latin word meaning *'I believe,'* and is a great doctrine for the entire company to rally behind. As an example, I have used the following credo for years due to its powerful message: *"The success of <our company> is dependent upon the quality and performance of our people. As an employee, I am the company's most valuable resource. I am dedicated to upholding our cultural beliefs, to providing service excellence to clients, partners, and colleagues and to developing innovative solutions. I am committed to embracing change and* *promoting an inclusive ethical business environment that fosters teamwork. It is through our dedicated efforts to build a diverse and inclusive work environment that we can exceed our customer's expectations with integrity and outstanding results."*

(more on the *'Board Pitch Book'* topic in Chapter 12: *'Available Options and Services to Build Your Board'*)

When interviewing Board candidates, first and foremost look for passion and interest in the organization's values, vision, and mission. I have personally become wary of Board candidates who, in their first 3 - 5 questions or comments, don't directly address the company's values or simply never address them at all throughout any discussions. This is a bellwether pointing to a lack of fundamental governance knowledge and almost certainly a seed for future misalignment of interests.[24]

The principle of initially laser-focusing efforts on Board candidate evaluation based on company values, vision, and mission is beautiful in its simplicity. It allows for a deep look into a Board candidate's psyche and the reasons for what they do. Getting back to the concept that Board Directorship is a formal career and a discipline, this secret weapon line-of-questioning, when delved into early on in the process, can save much time and effort in evaluating and selecting the proper Board candidates.

An example of how a company's culture starts with the Board is painfully obvious with the blatant instances of *'values erosion'* relating to the transportation and ridesharing company, Uber.

As the company's problems became more public, in February of 2017 a video surfaced of Travis Kalanick, the billionaire CEO and Board Member of Uber, berating an Uber driver during a pricing discussion. The driver, visibly agitated, mentions how he's lost $97,000 and is now bankrupt from what he states is Uber's *"flawed business strategy."* Kalanick, exhibiting an obvious low emotional intelligence (EQ) and lack of mindfulness intelligence (MQ), ends the discussion by angrily stating, *"Some people don't like to take responsibility for their own shit. They blame everything in their life on somebody else. Good luck!"* Even if Kalanick's statement could have contained some truth, his response was that of an immature business leader with an obvious need for leadership training. What better way to bury your business, and its reputation, than to berate and belittle your workers - the same ones that elevated him to billionaire status.

Then, in an effort to show Board and C-Level alignment across the company, an *'all-hands'* meeting, a town-hall-like gathering for employees, was called to address topics including the recently announced CEO's leave of absence (and subsequent resignation), news coverage on the company, and claims relating to gender discrimination. What happened next cannot be made up... First, Liane Hornsey, Uber's Human Resources Chief, asked everyone in attendance to hug each other. Yes, a request for some physical contact in a company meeting - somewhat of a risky move and in poor timing for a company mired in sexual harassment lawsuits - and from the head of HR? Next, Arianna Huffington, an Uber Board member, was speaking to the company in that same *'all hands'* meeting on the topic of building a more diverse board in an effort to spark change from the top. *"There's a lot of data that shows when there's one woman on a board, it's much more likely that there will be a second woman on the board,"* she stated to the group. That's when another Board member, David Bonderman, chimed in to joke, *"Actually, what it shows is that it's much more likely to be more talking."* Wow! A sexist joke at a company meeting designed to show support on changing a sexist environment... and from a Board member, no less. Needless to say, Bonderman's resignation in less than 24 hours was a welcomed response for many.

Uber -/ˈuːbə/: denoting an outstanding or supreme example of a particular kind of person or thing. To a great or extreme degree.

Even the definition of the word Uber as compared to the company is ironic. Setting a *'supreme example'* is a lofty goal and I admire this - likely a phrase that fits perfectly into any company's values, vision, or mission statements, not to mention the company's credo. But what could have happened differently at Uber? And where could a course correction have emanated from when earlier warning signs of a wayward company culture were starting to stray?

It begins and ends with the Board...

A common challenge for Boards, especially in the private sector, is the open and honest communication regarding development and focus areas for the Board and the CEO. This can be a tough conversation in public companies, too, however private companies have the added nuance of the CEO typically directing the Board or having overriding voting power on the Board. Tricky maneuvering, indeed, and territory that requires finesse and an ego-free exchange. All Boards should consider multiple facets of evaluation for the entire Board and the CEO that should not just be *'scheduled events'* or *'formal reviews,'* but more so ongoing analysis via observation with more frequent verbal feedback. (When this vetting can be started prior to Board Member appointment, even better.) Experience has shown that Board Members and CEOs who are open to this type of constructive feedback, and act on it, experience increased company performance, higher employee job satisfaction, ethical company-wide behaviors, lowered legal risks, decreased employee turnover, and a further sense of team members having found the right professional *'home'* - all of which are uber-important to any business.

For instances where a Board is in-place and already established, it is absolutely possible to realign its culture based on this values, vision, and mission approach. Similar exercises that have been mentioned for Board candidates can be implemented for seated Board Members through infusion into yearly review processes and integration during formal Board meetings (as well as Board Committee meetings). For Boards where I am the Chairman, I typically institute the practice of including a page in the meeting Board Book, preferably the first page, that includes the company's values, vision, and mission. I don't always read through all three sections during the Board meeting, but I do prefer to have one of the company values highlighted to be showcased for that particular meeting. In the Board meeting, a simple overview of that one company value offers an approach of consistently keeping the company values alive. Additionally, a request of any Board Member to give an example of that particular value being witnessed in another Board Member's actions has generated amazing responses and can further the bond between Board Members. Conversely, scenarios where the company or Board has not lived up to its core values can lead to amazing and worthwhile discussions, too. Referencing Roy E. Disney's quote, *"It's not hard to make decisions when you know what your values are,"* its also not hard to remedy scenarios where values have been breached, as long as they are discussed in an open and respectful environment.

Culture Fact: On average, less than half of employees know their company's mission, vision, and cultural values...[24a]

Mark A. Pfister

Part III

Mark A. Pfister

8   CREATING YOUR *'SPHERE OF INFLUENCE'* MODEL

"The greater is our sphere of influence, the greater the responsibility."

- Radhanath Swami

So, what exactly is meant by *'creating'* your Board's *'Sphere of Influence?'* This refers to your Board's industry & industry vertical diversity and experience. You can think of your Sphere of Influence (actual Board Members) as including chosen skill sets in <u>vertical</u> orientations. I am a proponent of having Board Member representation from numerous industries at the table, not just those with direct experience in your company's industry or industry vertical. Some of the best strategic plans for Boards I serve on, consult, or advise have been created and expanded upon through the melding of concepts from multiple, and sometimes disparate, industries. This diversity is extremely powerful and can catapult a company forward exponentially. Don't make the mistake of creating a team of *mini-me's* all with the same background and experience. You will essentially be creating a bubble of intelligence that is insulated from the rest of the world's best practices and devoid of other industry advancements - a dangerous proposition in these times of fast change, where quick adaptability can be one of the keys to survival.

To start, the components of your Sphere of Influence should always consider three parts:

- The skill set & expertise needs of your ideal board members,

- The industry & vertical experience needs of your ideal board members, and

- The current stage of growth of your company along with growth aspirations.

These considerations should be continuously evaluated throughout the Board build or Board rebuild process with an eye towards which phase of growth the company is in. In many cases, different phases of company growth bring about varying requirements and needed expertise in Board Directors.

Figure 21A: Common Company Growth Phases

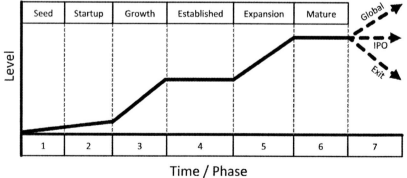

Know your current business stage of growth and build your Board accordingly. Consider if you need specific skill sets and experience for transitional times in your growth plan, or a core team through the entire lifecycle. It is common for companies to change Board Members, or supplement the Board with additional Board Members as a company enters a new phase of growth requiring additional, or different expertise needs. Other options include supplementing your core Board with Board Advisors to guide through each transitional period. These are not easy decisions, but know that you have options.

With that information, let's now incorporate the basic concept of your Board's Sphere of Influence and then move to populated examples.

In its simplest form, the Sphere of Influence concept allows for structured consideration of each Board Member's core leadership competency, operations competency, and skill set competencies.

Figure 22:[25] Foundational Sphere of Influence

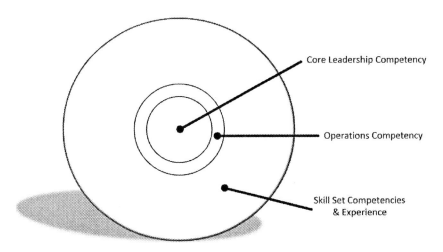

By showing this concept in concentric rings, we can visualize starting our thought process of the evaluation at the center and working our way outward. Yes, there is some simultaneity in this process. After all, you are no doubt thinking about a Board Member/candidate's Skill Set Competencies and Operations Competency at the same time you are sizing up Core Leadership Competency, however, there is value in systematically thinking about each area as a stand-alone competency to allow for directed and unbiased evaluations of each aptitude. It is in your interest to be shrewd and judicious in these steps to ensure proper vetting. The importance of this foundational step cannot be stressed enough. It is the platform on which the culture and effectiveness of your Board is built.

Figure 23:[25] Sphere of Influence – Core Leadership Competency

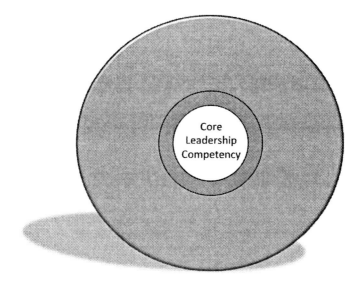

Ask a group of people the definition of true leadership and you will likely get a wide variance in response. This is because leadership is relative to the level within an organization, as well as the competency and approach of past leadership experienced. In contrast, when it comes to Board leadership, the answer can be quite specific due to its compartmentalized nature. An excellent shortlist of great Board leadership traits includes the following actions:[26]

- Mobilize action to further the values, vision, and mission of the organization,

- Help the organization adapt to a changing environment and ever-evolving outside forces,

- Anticipate and respond to crisis,

- Identify opportunities for change, growth, and transformation,

- Create future leaders.

When evaluating each Board Member or Board Candidate's Core Leadership Competency, aim to get definitive answers to the questions of whether or not they have:

- Proven deep experience in strategy creation?

- Shown skill in proper and effective governance?

- Successfully led large teams?

- Demonstrated an ability to motivate team members?

- Shown *great leader* traits of clear vision, courage, integrity, honesty, and humility?

Remember, just because someone may have previous Board experience, this does not automatically make them an effective or seasoned Board Director and leader. Make the determined and judicious effort to discern between the two in your evaluations.

Figure 24:[25] Sphere of Influence – Operations Expertise

It is becoming increasingly common for executives to claim deep leadership knowledge and experience, but lack significantly in the area of operations or the ability to *'operationalize'* a strategy or plan. In other words, a leader that is able to direct high-level actions, but not able to fully conceptualize, guide, or accomplish a successful end-to-end implementation as it pertains to governance of the process. This is dangerous territory for Boards, as having only half of the needed end-to-end expertise can lead to stalled company performance and constant redirection. Remember, a Board's role is to provide consistent and valuable input/direction to a CEO throughout all phases of a company's growth, strategy, and planning. A Board Director, or overall Board, that lacks deep operations experience is a red flag and does not fulfill this crucial requirement.

When evaluating the operations component of an existing Board Member, or those of a Board candidate, get definitive answers to the following questions:

- Do they have proven deep experience in implementing

complex strategies?

- Have they created and implemented effective governance mechanisms to monitor progress, successes, and failures?
- Have they shown an ability to *'right-size'* their strategies to the specific organization's priorities, capabilities, and size?
- Did they consistently and quickly adapt their strategy to changing environments and delivery challenges?

Taking the approach of alternating questions between strategic and tactical scenarios can be very helpful in understanding a Board Member/candidate's experience and abilities in the operations space. Always confirm that the level of Board Member leadership is accounting for the *'noses in, fingers out'* approach to ensure proper understanding and involvement.

Figure 25:[25]   Sphere of Influence – Skill Set Competencies & Experience

Another important exercise is determining which *'Skill Set Competencies & Experience'* are most important to your company. Remember, above and beyond your company's client-offering expertise, depending on what industry vertical your company is

in, there are important operations and internal company expertise considerations that should not be ignored. Considerations should include evaluating:

- Finance expertise
- Technology expertise
- Marketing expertise
- Legal expertise
- Human Resources / Human Capital expertise
- Sales expertise

The *'Skill Set Competencies & Experience'* focal point in the Sphere of Influence is typically the first, and sometimes only, area that an inexperienced company focuses on when building or rebuilding their Board. A lack of regard for *'Core Leadership Competency'* and *'Operations'* expertise possessed by all Board Members as a holistic evaluation has stymied many Boards, and companies, from reaching their full and intended potential. Don't make this mistake. It can be quite costly.

Figure 26:25 Sphere of Influence – Organization Example 1

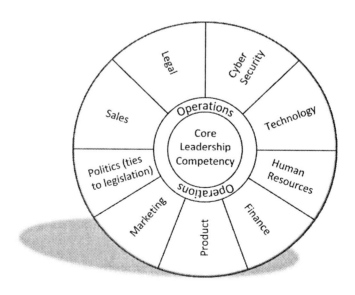

In this actual example implemented for an organization in the technology sector, a clear strategy has been established regarding the most important expertise areas needed for success at a specific company growth phase.

It should not be assumed in this example that each expertise *'pie slice'* corresponds to an individual Board Member – this could drastically and unnecessarily increase the size of your Board. The first and foremost concern is to understand the need for expertise, then ascertain whether certain skill sets can be *'grouped'* under a single Board Member. Do this with caution, however, as you don't want to undermine a needed expertise area in an effort to lessen the size of your Board. For this example technology company, we were able to *'group'* the Board Member expertise areas of Sales and Marketing as well as Technology and Cybersecurity making the Board seat count a total of 7 instead of 9.

This example also includes an interesting and innovative approach of including a well-known ex-politician on the Board. In the example, which is the case for many technology companies, existing and in-progress (yet publicly-released) legislation can have an incredibly positive effect on a company by supporting the creation of offerings that directly serve an existing or future client need. This technology company was able to leverage certain mandates of the Dodd Frank Act and more recent GDPR regulations, as it pertained to data security and protection, to create very valuable and timely service offerings. This knowledge and expertise was deemed imperative to meet a strategic requirement of differentiation as well as exponential growth aspirations.

Consideration for phase of growth (previous Fig. 21A) also directly plays a role in a determining the required skill set(s) within a *'Skill Set Competency and Experience'* category in your Sphere of Influence. Using the Finance Board Member position as an example, if your company is in its early stages of existence, finance expertise in the areas of forecasting, budgeting, tracking, reporting and other early-stage 'operations' focus areas are extremely important. It is likely that this particular Finance Board Member would need to have early-stage company experience, an understanding of a bootstrapping environment, and capital-raising experience. Conversely, that same Finance Board Member seat at mid or later stages of an organization's existence may be most valuable to the company they serve by having deep expertise and experience with M&A and/or IPO knowledge. Expertise is relative to a company's current position and must be considered at each growth phase of a business. These correlations can be made across the private, public and nonprofit Board space, as they each will experience many of the common company growth phases, perhaps just on a different scale. A reminder in the public board space, where existing Board Members are currently seated, the addition of Board Advisors may have to be leveraged to meet the required expertise and knowledge inputs.

Figure 27:[25] Sphere of Influence – Organization Example 2

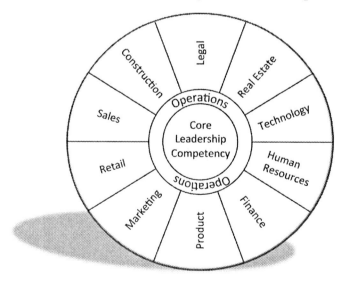

This Sphere of Influence model illustrates a very large range of expertise and experience designed to cover multiple business growth phases. Additionally, a wide range of industry coverage was decided to be extremely valuable to the organization in an effort to ensure *'diversity of perspective'* – more on this concept shortly.

Figure 28:[25] Sphere of Influence – Organization Example 3

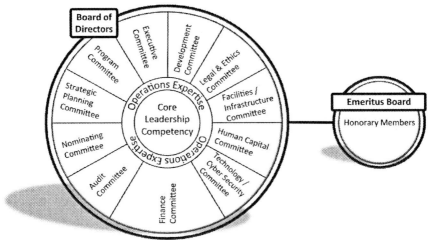

This Sphere of Influence model, correlated to numerous nonprofit organizations, addresses multiple skill set and experience areas typically required for long-term nonprofit success. These have been grouped by Board Committee in this example with the *'Skill Set Competencies & Experience'* covered by the lead, or Chair, of each expertise area. Although we will get into more detail on Board Committees in Chapter 11, there are some unconventional and notable mentions in this example:

- Program Chair/Committee: Ensure that the services and offerings of the nonprofit are relevant to their mission and able to quickly adapt programs to changing times and needs.
- Development Chair/Committee: Ensure focused, consistent and relevant efforts targeting existing, as well as potential, donors and sponsors.

- Facilities/Infrastructure Chair/Committee: Ensure that all facilities, buildings and infrastructure are in shape to support the nonprofit's operations with a firm plan for maintenance and expansion.
- Emeritus Board: In an effort to keep previous Board Members, many of which hold key relationships and connections, involved and benefiting the organization, Emeritus (or *'retired'* Board Members) can be very beneficial to long-term nonprofit success.

Nonprofits, due to their public-service nature, have many beneficial concepts that can be leveraged by private and public Boards to keep a service-focused vision. It is recommended that even if your organization is not a nonprofit, or if nonprofit Board service is not in your future, take the time to study nonprofit Board structure and techniques to ultimately benefit your Board.

A topic that may seem to be blatantly missing from the overall Sphere of Influence concept is the belief that public Boards, as well as private company Boards where Private Equity (PE) Board Members are to be assigned, don't have the luxury of following the Sphere of Influence model. To this I say *"it depends."*

Public companies frequently have the opportunity to replace Board Members due to mandatory retirement stipulations as well as term limits. These scenarios allow for unique opportunities to initiate a Sphere of Influence study. By creating profiles of the most needed experience and expertise for a company's current, or future phase of growth, the ideal Board composition can be achieved, or at least put on a path for future Board balance. The key is to simply start the process and then follow through.

Similarly, when reviewing private companies that are in the process of taking on PE capital infusions, there is a unique opportunity to *'weigh in'* on what experience would be ideal in the to-be-placed PE Board Members. I am reminded of an interesting experience when I was hired to architect a Board for a company. They successfully attracted a PE company during the process. We deliberately shared with the PE firm our in-process plans to ensure a proper Board Sphere of Influence and what experience areas would be most valuable. The PE firm agreed with the concept and assigned two Board Members that directly filled the needed requirements of two open Sphere of Influence expertise areas, also matching the needed growth phase experience. This turned out to be a great win for both the company and the PE firm, by simultaneously supporting a well-rounded strategy and further ensuring protection of investment.

When detailing the Sphere of Influence concept, Board structure must additionally be considered. Specifically, the options of a Board of Directors, Board of Advisors, or a combination of the two.

Figure 29:[25] Sphere of Influence – Structuring Option 1

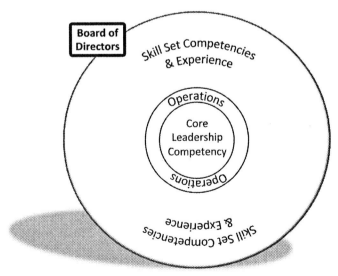

Boards of public, private and nonprofit organizations will typically have all of the most important expertise and experience areas *'in house'* as Board Directors.

Figure 30:[25] Sphere of Influence – Structuring Option 2

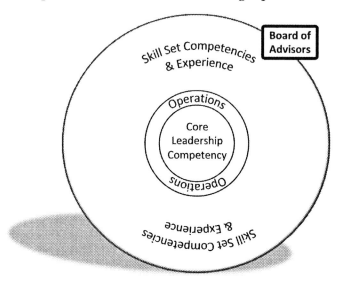

Some private companies opt to initiate their Board process by first assigning a team of Board Advisors. The same Sphere of Influence process can be utilized for this process.

Figure 31:[25] Sphere of Influence – Structuring Option 3

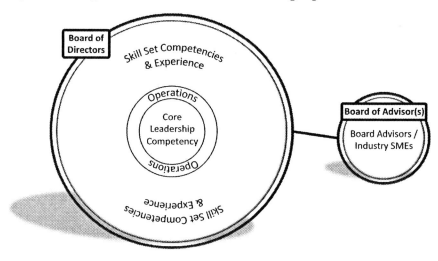

A hybrid model of a Board of Directors operating with a Board of Advisors for needed expertise is commonly seen throughout public, private, and nonprofit organizations.

Figure 32:[25] Sphere of Influence – Structuring Option 4

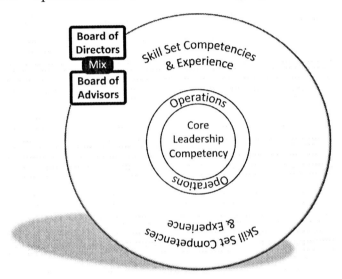

Some private and nonprofit organizations create a mix of Board Directors and Board Advisors, all considered to be somewhat *'seated'* Members, with certain operational delineations. This model has some limitations due to voting vs. non-voting members as well as some risk as it applies to insurance caveats, but every Member receives the same information and can weigh-in on decisions. This model requires very detailed minutes documenting fiduciary Members' *'voting'* vs. non-fiduciary Members' *'advice.'* A dedicated and savvy Board Secretary is highly recommended to document processes and outcomes in this model.

Additional Sphere of Influence considerations

Their exists a seemingly universal affinity for companies to search and appoint Board Members who are overwhelmingly from the same industry, not to mention the same industry vertical. It is possible that Boards have become more aligned with '*diversity*' solely as it applies to individual Board candidates' physical attributes and geographical ancestry, all the while overlooking industry diversity. Multiple recent experiences where I have been engaged to perform Board assessments have exposed a major lack of industry diversity - and the companies served by these clone-Boards have suffered.

Industry Vertical: Companies that serve specialized needs and that do not serve a broader market. An industry vertical market is tightly focused on meeting the needs of a specific area (vertical) within one industry.

Not only do I advocate for various *industry vertical* expertise in your Board architecture, I prefer various overall *industry* expertise on your Board - in other words, Boards that have members from other industries different from a company's present industry should be welcomed. This may seem counterintuitive, but the perspective and norm from other industries can offer up competitive advantages and prevent an insulated viewpoint within your company. With the speed of change in today's business environments, knowledge of emerging concepts and approaches, potentially incubated in other industries, could be the difference between your company's success or failure.

Disclaimer: I have frequently been harsh in many of my previous writings on a host of topics relating to nonprofit Boards due to a persistent disregard for proper Board decorum in both architecture and operations. However, when it comes to industry diversity, nonprofit Boards actually lead the pack over private and public company Boards. This is likely due to the typically more abstract approach to appointing nonprofit Board seats, but nevertheless it has proven to ensure Board industry diversity in many of these organizations.

Make a focused effort to ensure proper Core Leadership Competencies, Operations Expertise, and Skill Set Competencies & Experience in your Board design – these foundational *'Sphere of Influence'* elements are vital to your Board's long term success.

Template: For help in creating your Sphere of Influence model, reference *'Figure 50: Sphere of Influence / Planes of Congruence Template'* following the Notes & Quotes section at the end of this book.

Mark A. Pfister

9 INFUSING *'PLANES OF CONGRUENCE'* IN YOUR BOARD DESIGN

"Character is the real foundation of all worthwhile success."
- John Hays Hammond

Above and beyond industry and industry vertical expertise included in the design of your Board (mentioned in the previous chapter: *'Creating Your Sphere of Influence Model,'* pertaining to vertical considerations), Board member composition for your team should additionally be evaluated at multiple *'planes,'* or <u>horizontal</u> considerations, spanning across the entire Board makeup. These horizontal planes add depth to your board by creating additional *'character'* starting with the individual Board members and effectively encompassing the entire Board as a single operational entity.

These horizontals, or as I call them, *'Planes of Congruence,'* provide initial and additional evaluation criteria for Board candidates, as well as offer further structure for in-place Boards. In my personal experience, it is amazing how many existing Boards, or those in the process of being built, simply stop at unfinished portions of the previous *Sphere of Influence* step. These organizations have failed to infuse *'character'* into their Board, which in many cases leads to stagnant interaction and sub-par performance. We all know the *'brilliant jerk'* or the passive-aggressive type – not shining examples of ideal Board Members – but in scenarios where only skill set or background is evaluated, it is easy for toxic Board candidates to slip into a seat. Remember that it only takes a single toxic Board member to infect the entire Board, damaging camaraderie and lowering collective Board performance.

A series of visuals of the Planes of Congruence concept is helpful and it is something that I continually reference to this day when building Board teams. Think of it as a sort of fluid worksheet. Remember that the order of topics of this book are in a logical chronology of events, so this would be an exercise to commit to once you have completed your previous Sphere of Influence exercise, but before making any final decisions on Board candidates.

The following diagram shows the base Planes of Congruence model in its earliest and simplest visual form. We will build it out and populate an example from here.

Figure 33: Step 1 - Base Planes of Congruence Model[27]

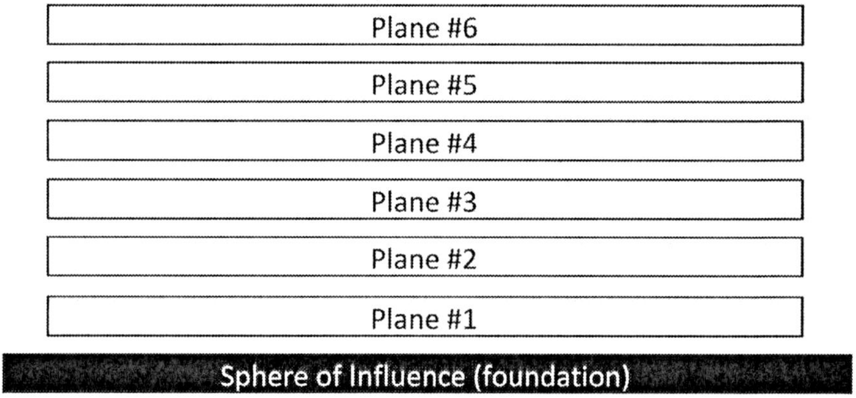

Plane #6
Plane #5
Plane #4
Plane #3
Plane #2
Plane #1
Sphere of Influence (foundation)

Before we define our example Planes of Congruence, note how the previous vertical Sphere of Influence exercise output has been laid down horizontally to now sit as the foundation of our Planes of Congruence exercise. We are essentially building on top of the detailed Sphere of Influence foundational element of the design with additional and worthwhile Board Member *'character'* considerations. The total number of *'planes'* is up to you and your defined criteria for Board inclusion.

Some required horizontal qualities, as we will see in a moment, will be expectations for all Board Members to bring to the table or adhere to. It is important to note, however, that not all Planes of Congruence will span across the entire Board as they are not necessarily suggested as single *'fit'* requirements for all Board Members. In building balance on your Board, under a specific Planes of Congruence requirement, you may require a host of *'personalities'* or a mix of *'age/experience'* perspective. Planes of Congruence categories allow you to evaluate these considerations and requirements to construct your ideal Board's makeup.

Figure 34:   Step 2 – Example Semi-Populated Planes of Congruence Model[27]

Plane #6: Common Vertical Knowledge + Varying Industry Backgrounds
Plane #5: Emotional Intelligence (EQ)
Plane #4: Personality Traits
Plane #3: Diversity - Women to Men Ratio
Plane #2: Age Range / Generational Span
Plane #1: Strategy & Governance Expertise
Sphere of Influence (foundation)

Furthering the population of our example company Board, a total of six Planes of Congruence considerations have been agreed to formulate the perfect Board makeup for this company. Referencing a previous point, Planes 1 and 5 are uniform requirements of all Board Members. Planes 2, 3, 4 and 6 are guidelines of variance to ensure balance and perspective across members of the Board.

Figure 35: Step 3 - Example Populated Planes of Congruence Model[27]

Plane #6: Common Vertical Knowledge / Varying Industry Backgrounds – Services Business (min. 2/3) / < 25% Industry Overlap
Plane #5: Emotional Intelligence (EQ) – Highly Experienced
Plane #4: Personality Traits – Balance: Analyst, Diplomat, Sentinel, Explorer
Plane #3: Diversity - Women to Men Ratio – Minimum 30% Women
Plane #2: Age Range / Generational Span – 35 to 80 Years of Age
Plane #1: Strategy & Governance Expertise - Required
Sphere of Influence (foundation)

The fully populated Planes of Congruence model for our example company is now complete with measures of success defined:

Plane #1: Agreed that all Board Members, regardless of their Sphere of Influence fit, are required to have significant Strategy & Governance expertise.

Plane #2 : Agreed that there will be a large Age Range / Generational span on this Board ranging from the youngest age of 35 up to the age of 80. When a Board contains multiple age groups across multiple generations, wow. What a powerhouse. This dynamic environment is what you are looking for, as long as you have created an environment for each generation to thrive. An additional note on this concept is the value of potentially staggered retirement Board seat vacancies.

Plane #3: Agreed that the Diversity of Women to Men Ratio will be a minimum of 30% women on the Board. Male/Female balance is a big consideration for a Board - and I don't mean this as a *'quota'* type of connotation. The most successful Boards I serve as a Board Member, consult, or advise, have a noticeable balance of men and women. These Boards just simply *'work'* better... and the data from numerous studies supports this. Combining gender diversity with industry diversity elevates *'diversity of perspective,'* something extremely important to the companies that Boards serve. *'Diversity of perspective,'* leading to *'diversity of thought,'* is an important conduit to create in strategic positions - and this needs to be paramount in Board architecture considerations to ensure outstanding company results.

Plane #4: Agreed that there will be a balance of Personality Traits across the following categories to ensure diverse viewpoints and approaches to decisions and challenges:

- *'Analyst'* type
- *'Diplomat'* type
- *'Sentinel'* type
- *'Explorer'* type

Diversity once again is the name of the game. For every *'Adventurer'* have a *'Logistician.'* For every *'Entrepreneur'* have an *'Executive.'* For every *'Advocate'* have a *'Protagonist.'* For best results, balance your personality types across Analyst types, Diplomat types, Sentinel types and Explorer types.

Plane #5: Agreed that every Board Member, regardless of their Sphere of Influence fit, is required to have an extremely refined Emotional Intelligence (EQ) and response mechanism. Emotional

Intelligence, a.k.a. EI or EQ, is defined as *'the capacity to be aware of, control, and express one's emotions, and to handle interpersonal relationships judiciously and empathetically.'*[28] This has become much more important in today's society when the topic of who you voted for or what flavor ice cream you prefer can result in supermarket fist fights. ...And yes, there are ways to measure someone's EQ as well as the Board team's collective EQ (known as TQ). More on this in Chapter 13, *'Board Member Evaluation & Selection.'*

Plane #6: Agreed that Common Vertical Knowledge / Varying Industry Backgrounds will adhere to the following requirements:

- 2/3rds of Board Members will have in-depth experience and knowledge in services-based businesses and correlated services-industry practices.
- To ensure diversity of thought, there will be no more than 25% of the entire makeup of the Board previously or currently involved in the company's industry vertical.

These are just a few of many additional Planes of Congruence considerations you can evaluate when building or rebuilding your Board. A current baseline list of horizontal Planes of Congruence I consider for evaluation in all Board builds includes:

- Deep Strategy understanding
- Deep Governance experience
- Age range
- Generational span
- Women/Men diversity
- Race/Nationality diversity
- Personality trait balance
- Intelligence/vertical background (IQ) *

- Emotional Intelligence (EQ) *

- Team Intelligence (TQ) (as a group) *

- Mindfulness Intelligence (MQ) *

- Varying industry backgrounds

- Fluency/geography familiarity

- Introvert/extrovert

* see more on these topics in upcoming Chapter 13 – 'Board Member Evaluation & Selection'

You will no doubt add a few of your own Planes of Congruence requirements and considerations in your Board build or Board rebuild aspirations. This frequently overlooked step will reap huge rewards in the effectiveness of your Board.

Template: For help in creating your Planes of Congruence model, reference 'Figure 50: Sphere of Influence / Planes of Congruence Template' following the Notes & Quotes section at the end of this book.

Mark A. Pfister

10 BOARD MEMBER COVERAGE & BALANCE

"The present is the equilibrium of the past and the future."
                                                    - Charles de Leusse

Similar to your Planes of Congruence creating the *'character'* of your Board, the *'Coverage and Balance'* of your Board, as it correlates to Board Member's expertise and experience, creates the *'depth'* of your Board. Depth is an important characteristic of Boards as it offers relevant guidance and deeper thought processes leading to more effective deliberation on important Board topics and strategies.

In essence, Board Member Coverage and Balance refers to two basic concepts:

- Coverage: Ensuring that you have engaged at least one true expert in each of your designed Sphere of Influence areas on your Board, while also meeting your Planes of Congruence requirements.

- Balance: A strategic and predetermined overlap of expertise and experience as it relates to your Board's Sphere of Influence areas, while also meeting your Planes of Congruence requirements.

A series of visuals on this topic are helpful to fully illustrate this important Board concept.

Figure 36: Coverage - Example Expertise Coverage Analysis

Sphere of Influence Area	Technology	Human Resources	Finance	Product	Marketing	Sales	Legal
Board Member 1	(1)	3	3	2	3	3	4
Board Member 2	4	4	3	2	(1)	2	4
Board Member 3	3	2	(1)	4	4	2	3
Board Member 4	4	2	2	4	3	3	(1)
Board Member 5	2	4	3	3	2	(1)	2
Board Member 6	3	3	(1)	3	4	3	2
SME Coverage	✔	✗	✔	✗	✔	✔	✔
Knowledge Depth	→	↓	↑	↓	→	↑	↑

1 = Subject Matter Expert (SME) / 2 = Deep Knowledge / 3 = Operational Knowledge / 4 = Minimal Knowledge

Coverage: In the example company represented in Figure 36, let's first align on where this company is at in their Board build, or Board evaluation/ rebuild process:

- Sphere of Influence: This Board is designed for needed expertise and experience in 7 areas including technology, human resources, finance, product, marketing, sales and legal.

- Planes of Congruence: Although not represented in this Coverage and Balance exercise, it is assumed that all Board Members or Board candidates have met or fit the predetermined requirements of a previous Planes of Congruence exercise.

- Size of Board: This Board is designed for a total of 6 Board Members with *'grouping'* of only two Sphere of Influence Skill Set and Experience areas within one Board Member (6 Board Members across 7 Sphere of Influence areas).

- Board Committees: The creator of this Board is interested in having each Board Member also serve as the Chair of their correlating expertise Committee area (more on this in Chapter 11, *'The Importance of Board Committees'*).

Now that the basis is set, let's look at where we are at specifically relating to *'coverage'* of all Sphere of Influence Skill Set Competencies and Experience areas (referencing Figure 36):

- Technology: Board Member 1 has been evaluated to meet the criteria of the Sphere of Influence as a Subject Matter Expert (SME).

- Finance: Board Member 3 and Board Member 6 have been evaluated to meet the criteria of the Sphere of Influence as Subject Matter Experts (SME).

- Marketing: Board Member 2 has been evaluated to meet the criteria of the Sphere of Influence as a Subject Matter Expert (SME).

- Sales: Board Member 5 has been evaluated to meet the criteria of the Sphere of Influence as a Subject Matter Expert (SME).

- Legal: Board Member 4 has been evaluated to meet the criteria of the Sphere of Influence as a Subject Matter

Expert (SME).

Notable Observations:

- Human Resources: Although this expertise and knowledge area has been deemed imperative through this example company's earlier Sphere of Influence exercise, they are currently lacking an SME.

- Product: This expertise and knowledge area, also deemed imperative through this example company's earlier Sphere of Influence exercise, is currently lacking an SME.

- Finance: This expertise and knowledge area has two SMEs associated with it. This is not necessarily a negative situation (as we will review next), but it could be limiting based on this example company's design criteria of six Board Members total.

- Currently, the example shows that only 5 Sphere of Influence SME areas are covered of a needed 7. Additionally, no current Board Member or Board candidate is able to meet the criteria of 'grouping' two Sphere of Influence Skill Set and Experience areas within one Board Member to satisfy the design of 6 Board Members total.

This simple study tells us that the example company is not currently on track to meet the Board's 'Coverage' requirements specifically relating to their Sphere of Influence design. A second attempt would be required to fill the gaps of Human Resources and Product as well as evaluate which 2 areas are most easily grouped under 1 SME.

If you and I were existing Board Members of this example

company and weighing in on next steps, the following strategic recommendations would likely be made:

- Arguable, it is most likely that the easiest SME *'grouping'* that could be accomplished is between the Sphere of Influence areas of Sales and Marketing or Marketing and Product. Another option, if the assumption is that the example company is heavily weighted in the technology industry and producing products, would be to look at the option of grouping Technology & Product Sphere of Influence SME areas. Overall, the grouping exercise would be subjective and dependent on varying industry-specific and company-specific considerations.

- The immediate need to document a specific position description and requirements to initiate a Human Resources Board Director SME search.

- The immediate need to document a specific position description and requirements to initiate a Product Board Director SME search (or grouped SME search).

- Consider the possibility, due to potential time constraints or ability to locate an ideal Board candidate, of engaging a short-term or long-term Board Advisor to cover a missing SME area. This could be done as either an addition to the base design of 6 Board Members, or in place of a sixth Board Member.

Figure 37: Example Expertise Coverage Analysis - Balance

Sphere of Influence Area	Technology	Human Resources	Finance	Product	Marketing	Sales	Legal
Board Member 1	1	3	3	(2)	3	3	4
Board Member 2	4	4	3	(2)	1	(2)	4
Board Member 3	3	(2)	1	4	4	(2)	3
Board Member 4	4	(2)	(2)	4	3	3	1
Board Member 5	(2)	4	3	3	(2)	1	(2)
Board Member 6	3	3	1	3	4	3	(2)
SME Coverage	✔	✗	✔	✗	✔	✔	✔
Knowledge Depth	→	↓	↑	↓	→	↑	↑

1 = Subject Matter Expert (SME) / 2 = Deep Knowledge / 3 = Operational Knowledge / 4 = Minimal Knowledge

Balance: Furthering the evaluation of our example company's details, we need to investigate whether or not a strategic and predetermined overlap of expertise and experience has been instituted as it relates to the Board's Sphere of Influence areas.

Balance, somewhat referring to an *'overlap'* or *'backup'* of expertise in a Board's Sphere of Influence design, is very important for a Board. Why do we want a certain degree of expertise overlap on Boards? Once again, depth. Let's delve into what exactly the importance of depth is when it comes to its application on a Board and then we will compare this back to our example company evaluation.

SME depth on a Board offers immeasurable value:

- Eliminates one-sided and single-viewpoint proposals and decision-making by a sole Board Member SME that could effect a company for years into the future. Depth of knowledge and overlap in SME areas leads to deeper discussions and fully vetted outcomes.

- Allows for unconventional and expanded/varying industry considerations (referring back to multiple industry representation on your Board through your Planes of Congruence model).

- Fosters an open learning environment within your Board (many stagnant Boards experience lower Board Member camaraderie and satisfaction when they feel learning, or knowledge expansion is blocked).

- In cases where a Board Member is not able to attend a Board meeting, update meeting, or Committee Meeting, a predetermined and knowledgeable Board Member with background in the SME knowledge area can be prepped and able to lead the discussion. Due to a Board's somewhat limited *'together'* time, an absent Board Member and/or missing Committee Chair at a Board Meeting is no longer an excuse for no update, missed vote, or lack of progress.

With these considerations in mind, we will review our example company's *'depth'* as it relates to Balance. Figure 37 has the skill set knowledge areas of *'2'* circled, representing Deep Knowledge of existing Board Members (or Board candidates). Deep Knowledge is not quite the level of an SME, and may not even be a particular Board Member's *'day job'*, but it does show a deep knowledge and proficiency of that expertise area.

Preferably, each of a Board's Sphere of Influence areas, shown in the columns, would ideally have one SME (represented as a 1 on the chart) and two *'Deep Knowledge'* Board Members (represented as a 2 on the chart). In my experience, this guideline has a direct correlation to a Board's success and effectiveness through proper coverage and balance practices.

Directly evaluating the example company's depth in Figure 37 highlights some interesting observations (note that this is prior to any corrective actions as outlined in the earlier *'Coverage'* section of this chapter):

- Technology: An SME is represented, but only one *'Deep Knowledge'* Board Member, or Board candidate, is identified. A horizontal arrow in the *'Knowledge Depth'* row represents some level of depth coverage, but does not fully satisfy our criteria of two *'Deep Knowledge'* representatives supporting an *'SME'* on the Board.

- Human Resources: No SME is represented here, however, we do have two *'Deep Knowledge'* representatives. The *'SME Coverage'* row shows an 'x' identifying that we are missing an SME, so the *'Knowledge Depth'* row overall shows a downward facing arrow representing lack of compliance in our model within this Sphere of Influence area.

- Finance: Two SMEs are represented along with one *'Deep Knowledge'* representative. In theory, this would satisfy our *'Knowledge Depth'* requirement, hence the upward facing arrow.

- Product: No SME is represented here, however, we do have two *'Deep Knowledge'* representatives. The *'SME Coverage'* row shows an 'x' identifying that we are missing an SME, so the *'Knowledge Depth'* row overall shows a downward facing arrow representing lack of compliance in our model within this Sphere of Influence area.

- Marketing: An SME is represented, but only one *'Deep Knowledge'* Board Member, or Board candidate, is identified. A horizontal arrow in the *'Knowledge Depth'* row represents some level of depth coverage, but does not fully satisfy our criteria of two *'Deep Knowledge'* representatives on the Board within this Sphere of Influence area.

- Sales: One SME is represented along with two *'Deep Knowledge'* representative. This would satisfy our *'Knowledge Depth'* requirement, hence the upward facing arrow.

- Legal: One SME is represented along with two *'Deep Knowledge'* representative. This would satisfy our *'Knowledge Depth'* requirement, hence the upward facing arrow.

It should be clearly evident that just because an existing Board or a Board in the process of construction has seemingly passed the Sphere of Influence and Planes of Congruence phases, this does not necessarily ensure that the Board has proper Coverage and Balance. Performing a simple study of this nature can be quite illuminating by quickly pointing out important gaps requiring reassessment.

Create and track your own Board Member Coverage & Balance chart throughout your Board build, or Board rebuild, to ensure relevant guidance and deeper thought processes. Let the higher-level discussions and deliberations begin!

Board Fact: It isn't unusual for some of a company's Board of Directors to be tied to major vendors. This is done to strengthen important strategic relationships between the companies.

Mark A. Pfister

11 THE IMPORTANCE OF
BOARD COMMITTEES

"They sit there in committees day after day, and they each put in a color and it comes out gray. And we all have heard the saying, which is true as well as witty, that a camel is a horse that was designed by a committee."

- Allen Sherman

The general word *'committee'* has taken on an interesting and sometimes joke-like perception in recent years. It is frequently used to mock how slowly groups make decisions, and what the muddled outcome will likely be once a mass of people all incorporate what they believe are their absolutely critical ideas. Dating back to 1952, the saying that "*a camel is a horse designed by a committee*" even has its own Wiktionary page with the explanation, "*[this is] an expression critical of committees - or by analogy, group decision-making - by emphasizing the ineffectiveness of incorporating too many conflicting opinions into a single project. In this figure of speech, the distinguishing features of a camel, such as its humps and poor temperament, are taken to be deformities that resulted from its poor design.*"[29]

Comical, yes... but there is more than meets the eye with this explanation - supportive of the reasoning for creating smaller, more focused groups to more effectively and efficiently work through challenges, as well as proactive undertakings. Board Committees are designed to serve this purpose. Conversely, to have an entire Board work through all issues and endeavors creates a fractured environment that undermines the purpose of the Board by making it a tactical, instead of primarily strategic, group.

Figure 38: Benefits of Board Committees[30]

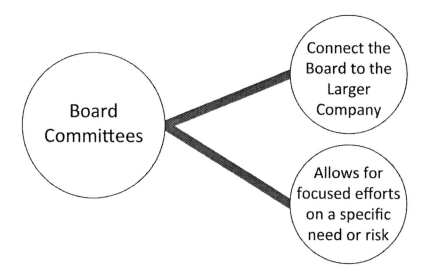

Board Committees, dedicated groups led by a Board Member (Committee Chair), are designed to take on challenges that fit into their specific expertise and experience areas, for offline discussion and solutioning. This approach, followed by a written report of findings, outcomes, and recommendations (sent out well in advance and to be voted on during a Board meeting) allows for the deserved structure and time for each topic to be properly addressed. This structural order is paramount for matters to be systematically investigated, vetted, and presented in a logical and formal manner. Many Boards make the mistake of performing a Board Committee's actions within the Board Meeting – this is improper Board decorum and drastically hinders a Board's progress.

Properly constructed and operational Board Committees have an additional, yet frequently overlooked, benefit to the companies they serve – connecting the Board to the larger company. It is quite common for Boards to become insulated from daily operations and the technical challenges that a company faces. After all, a *'noses in, fingers out'* approach, if not properly implemented or governed, can be somewhat limiting in rolling up true and useful information for the Board's consideration. This is not to say a CEO is not performing their job correctly in keeping the Board informed, but there are inherent *'connections'* that can be made through properly constructed Board Committees to aid in checks and balances for strategic decision-making. This is best illustrated through an actual example of how a specific Board Committee created a structured conduit for information sharing leading to increased company performance.

On a recent Board I was re-architecting for a large, well-known company, there was an obvious need to revamp, not only the structure of their Board Committees, but also the expectations, processes, and goals of existing and newly formed Board Committees. Following a detailed review of 3-year trending on major strategic decisions made by the company, along with their governance component effectiveness (of which formal Board Committees should have played an integral role), it became obvious that there was a major gap in their effectiveness. Poor company performance, by means of the Board's inadequate strategic guidance and governance of the CEO, was directly correlated to lacking Board Committee effectiveness. Make no mistake, the Board Committees, and subsequently the entire Board, are directly accountable to these outcomes.

The actions taken to remedy these shortcomings can be utilized as a structural roadmap in building or rebuilding Board Committees for any organization – private, public and nonprofit, or at the very least, spark creative and new approaches in your innovative and modern Board design. These steps and considerations, as applied in our actual example company, include:

- Trending of Previous 3-Year Overall Company Strategic Decision Making: By evaluating the company's performance over the previous 3 years, it was obvious that market share and relevance was decreasing. In my experience, this downward spiral is always attributed to inadequate strategy and fractured governance. First priority was a full revamp of the Strategic Planning Committee and the Governance Committee.

- Sphere of Influence Structure Evaluation: An immediate study of the Board's Sphere of Influence and Planes of Congruence was enacted to see if proper skill sets, as well as strategy and governance expertise, was present within the Board. It was not. These findings validated the speculation that there was inadequate strategic guidance and a fractured governance model within the Board, and in interaction with the CEO. Knowing that time was of the essence, and the desire to not hastily increase Board size with new Board Members, two Board Advisors were quickly engaged to lead the Strategic Planning Committee and Governance Committee. The decision was also made to embark on a 1 year plan, to be prioritized in the strategic plan, to rebuild the Board with the depth needed to operate efficiently and effectively.

- Board Committee Structure: Ideally, inclusion of at least 1 knowledgeable Board Member in addition to the

Committee Chair (assumed to be a Board Member and SME) is highly recommended in all Board Committees. Referencing back to our *'Board Member Coverage & Balance'* model in Chapter 10, specifically *'Figure 37: Example Expertise Coverage Analysis – Balance,'* a properly constructed overall Board should have at least one, preferably 2, *'Deep Knowledge'* Board Members in each Sphere of Influence area in addition to an SME. In most cases, the Sphere of Influence *'Skill Set Competencies & Experience'* areas can and should be correlated to actual Board Committees. This will make the requirement of all Board Committees containing a Board Member SME and at least 1 *'Deep Knowledge'* Board Member quite easy to accomplish. Note that the inclusion of an SME and at least 1 *'Deep Knowledge'* member on each Board Committee allows for investigation, deliberation, vetting and option-decisioning to be successfully accomplished outside the boardroom, for later Board voting. Further to this point, an important rule of thumb to keep in mind is that *"Board meetings should begin where Board Committee and Board Member preparation ends."* In our example company, we prioritized strategic planning and governance to immediately have an impact.

- Board Committee Structure: Inclusion of varying levels of company inputs by means of incorporating select company employees on Board Committees is an interesting and rewarding concept to consider. In the example company referenced, the VP of Services, responsible for carrying out the strategic plan through operational oversight, along with a Service Technician, were asked to join select Strategic Planning Committee meetings as informal advisors. They were essentially appointed and announced across the company as internal strategic advisors to the Board for a term of 2 quarters – and the resulting outcome was incredible. Not only did the Strategic Planning Committee get invaluable *'boots on the ground'* viewpoints from a manager and technician in the company's major revenue-generating division, but morale noticeably increased as measured by quarterly company surveys. Referencing back to Chapter 6: The Role of Governance, specifically *'Figure 12: Board Governance Framework,[18]'* morale is a foundational element in supporting company Values & Culture – and of major concern to the Board. The Service Technician, who became somewhat of a company celebrity, had unknowingly addressed an age-old challenge of employees commiserating about what leadership *'had decided'* or *'done to them,'* and gave them a mutually valuable voice. Additionally, the Service Technician became a collection point of other employees' ideas, concerns and innovations that could be represented through someone who fully understood the role and its inherent challenges. This Board was no longer viewed as a shadowy, secretive group, but a humanized, caring, knowledgeable and innovative instrument dedicated to company and employee success. Although not part of the original plan, we invited the VP and the Service Technician to represent specific areas of the Strategic Planning Committee presentation to the Board - another win for the overall organization. Note that this approach is somewhat unconventional, but remember that in this book we are addressing *modern* Board construction and operations, not old-school formats that can be limiting in their effectiveness and success. In addition to all customary duties, Boards also have an incredible opportunity to support and advance a company's Values & Culture that should not be underestimated or ignored.

• Processes and Procedures: The creation of a common Board Committee framework is equally important in the success and effectiveness of the entire Board. It is recommended to track topics that each Board Committee is working through with milestone dates assigned. There is great value in the very simple framework of tracking the 5 milestones of a) initiation, b) discovery, c) planning, d) implementation and e) operations for every topic or challenge undertaken by each Board Committee (more on this concept in Chapter 15). These milestones can then easily be addressed and prioritized within formal Board meetings and also incorporated within the strategic plan.

- Outcomes, Reporting and Information Dissemination: Further to the previous *'Processes and Procedures'* section, structured outcomes of Board Committee actions through formal reporting and information dissemination are key. Unfortunately, this is overlooked on many Boards. One-pager Board Committee report templates, incorporating all topics and focus areas being worked on by a Board Committee, work very well for this purpose. An effective and simple Board Committee reporting template format should include the following areas:

  o Short Executive Summary
  o Milestones met/delivered since last Board Meeting
  o Milestones scheduled for the period leading up to the next Board Meeting
  o Changes or updates to Milestone(s) delivery
  o Risks and Issues
  o Notable findings and outcomes
  o Areas requiring decisioning or voting by the Board
  o Strategic considerations
  o Reminder of Board Committee's actions in correlation to current agreed strategic plan

This Board Committee reporting process standardizes

response formats and allows for a view into operational, as well as strategic, areas of interest to the Board. It goes without saying that these reports should be sent out at least one week in advance of Board meetings to allow for review by the entire Board. During the Board meeting, the Chair of each committee, under the assumption that the entire report has already been reviewed by all Board members, should only address the areas requiring clarification (via questions from Board Members) for input or a vote. I also recommend that Committee Chairs call out any accolades of team members during each Board Committee update as a way of balancing challenges with triumphs - it is all too easy to focus only on the areas needing to be fixed and not those that have been conquered.

Boards that leverage these fundamental Board Committee approaches experience vastly greater company performance and increased morale across the organization. Additionally, CEOs are fully supported in their mission to guide and drive the organization forward, making their relationship with the Board even more valuable.

A great principle to remember when creating, rebuilding, or evaluating your Board Committees is the following simple assertion:

The Board Committee structure, as well as the Committee Chairs, *'make or break'* the effectiveness of the entire Board

Proper ongoing diligence should be dedicated to this principle to ensure your Board, and the overall company, is properly served.

Figure 39: Board Committee Purpose[30]

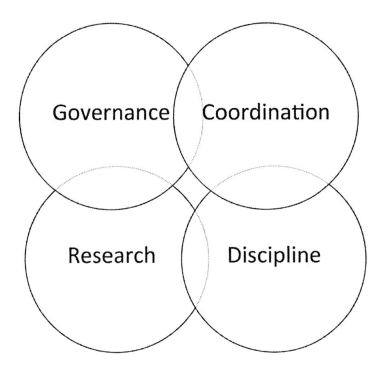

Furthermore, the proper application of governance, coordination, research, and discipline within Board Committees allows for Boards to:

- Distribute the work of the Board
- Accelerate outcomes through a *'divide and conquer'* approach
- Leverage specific talents, knowledge, and experience of Board Members
- Allow for wider participation by all Board Members

Board Committees frequently need to be reminded of these important responsibilities of their existence – and held accountable to effectual outcomes.

Figure 40: Standing Committees & Ad Hoc Committees[30]

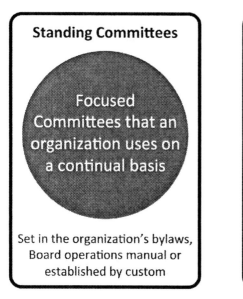

Standing Committees

Focused Committees that an organization uses on a continual basis

Set in the organization's bylaws, Board operations manual or established by custom

Ad Hoc Committees

Formed for a limited period of time to address a specific need

When the work of the Ad Hoc Committee is completed, the committee is dissolved

Offering further flexibility in your Board architecture and construction, Board Committees can be ongoing and permanent in nature, or enacted for specific endeavors. Standing Committees are focused committees that a Board leverages on an ongoing basis. These are typically firmly set within the organization's bylaws, Board operations manual, or simply established by custom. Conversely, Ad Hoc Committees are formed for a limited period of time to address a specific, or urgent need. When the work of the Ad Hoc Committee is completed, the committee is then disbanded.

Having the proper Board Committees, with proper Chairs, or leads, ensures that each challenge and proactive (and sometimes reactive) undertaking gets the laser focus and guidance it deserves. Note that you can properly evaluate candidates who would be successful in Committee Chair positions with the procedures mentioned in upcoming Chapter 13: *'Board Member*

Evaluation & Selection.'

Plan your committees carefully and know that these can change for different phases of growth, or specific business challenges. Although the actual number of committees and their titles can vary depending on organization size and purpose, this is an important effort to strategize whether evaluating an existing Board, or architecting a new Board. Many Boards in both the public and private sector incorporate Standing Committees including:

- Executive Committee
- Governance Committee
- Strategic Planning Committee
- Finance Committee
- Audit Committee
- Technology Committee
- Cybersecurity / Data Security Committee
- Compensation Committee
- Human Capital / HR Committee
- Personnel Committee
- Board Development Committee
- Leadership Development Committee
- Evaluation Committee
- Risk Committee
- Nominating Committee
- Marketing Committee
- Promotion & Sales Committee
- Public Relations Committee
- Product Development Committee
- Program Development Committee

Again, these Board Committees are typically referred to as Standing Committees, essentially denoting them as full-time and on-going committees.

The Non-Profit sector would likely include or substitute the following Standing Board Committees:

- Development Committee
- Campaign Committee (fundraising)
- Program Committee
- Event Committee
- Outreach / Membership Committee

Ad Hoc Committees, or temporary committees, could include:

- Audit Committee
- Ethics Committee
- Events Committee
- Nominating Committee
- Research Committee
- Fundraising Committee
- Steering Committee
- Board Development Committee

These Ad Hoc Committees are created to accomplish a specific goal and can then disband until needed again.

Certain Board Committees may change or have varying focus depending on company needs & stage of growth. All committees, either Standing or Ad Hoc, are mentioned as a matter of practice, but know that you can create committees for just about any area you deem important, for the long-term well-being of your company or organization.

For a Board to accomplish its duties effectively, it is essential that all Board Members understand and embrace their individual responsibilities specifically relating to the Board Committees they serve. Spend the needed time to structure and govern this important Board focus area.

Template: For help in aligning your Board Committees to your Sphere of Influence model, reference 'Figure 50: Sphere of Influence / Planes of Congruence Template' following the Notes & Quotes section at the end of this book.

Mark A. Pfister

Part IV

Mark A. Pfister

12 AVAILABLE OPTIONS & SERVICES TO BUILD YOUR BOARD

"If I don't know my options, I don't have any."

- Diana Korte

At this stage, you have evaluated your company's Values, Vision, and Mission, built your Sphere of Influence model, prioritized your Planes of Congruence considerations, ensured proper Board Coverage and Balance, and thought through your Board Committee structure - all in support of fostering a constructive environment and attracting and retaining great Board Director talent. If you are architecting a new Board, you will have to find the ideal Board members to support your strategy. If you are re-building an existing Board, your approach will likely include plans to replace, or add Board Members, or Board Advisors, to ensure proper support.

Today you have multiple options in building, or rebuilding the right Board team. These options range in efforts from internal search efforts (potentially being conducted by the Nominating Committee) to engaging professional search firms to hiring ready-built Board Advisor teams. Combining search efforts through multiple channels could also be an option to assist with breadth of search efforts and to shorten duration, assuming that there are no stipulations to the contrary within engaged professional search firm legal stipulations.

Figure 41: Opportunities to Acquire the Right Board Members[31]

Executive Search companies specializing in Board positions are always an option. Interestingly, in the 2016–2017 'NACD Public Company Governance Survey,'[34b] for the first time since NACD began to survey its members on this issue, formal search firms were the leading source public Boards used to identify their most recently recruited director. With Boards no longer primarily relying on personal networks to identify and recruit new directors, this trend is likely a nod to Boards wanting to reach a larger candidate network. Additionally, and potentially more importantly, this approach is likely pointing out the trending of Boards searching for more experienced and professional candidates. When utilizing formal search companies, increase the success rate of these types of searches by sharing your plan (Values/Vision/Mission, Sphere of Influence, Planes of

Congruence, etc.) with the search company, so they have multiple dimensions of what successful candidates look like for your organization.

Networking Groups can help to expose your needs to the proper individuals, too. Make your intentions clear and definitely mention that you have a detailed strategic plan to build a modern and effective Board. Word will travel fast...

Organizations and associations such as the National Association of Corporate Directors (NACD) and the American College of Corporate Directors (ACCD) have great outlets for identifying viable Board members, both in formal ways (through the organization), or informal ways (by attending events and forums for the purpose of networking).

Even LinkedIn has made Board Member searches quite simple, allowing you to laser-focus on your ideal candidates. Their search functionality has greatly improved. Pay special attention in using Boolean search criteria to quickly specialize and narrow down your searches. Also, for an example of a *'highly searchable'* LinkedIn Board Member profile with multiple Board search criteria buzz-words embedded, see mine here:

www.linkedin.com/in/markapfister/

Feel free to connect with me while you are there.

In all of the previous Board candidate search scenario options, always aim for at least three viable, final candidates for each open Board position. Anything less will not give the options needed for proper comparison and decision making. Know that if you identify a Board candidate through a informal channel, even while simultaneously utilizing a formal search company, you can put the candidate into the formal mix through the search company for proper and fair evaluation. Reach out to the search/placement company for them to do this coordination.

BaaS – For private companies, and in cases where available time to build a proper Board is scarce, the option of a fully-built and for-hire Board of Advisors can be the answer. This concept, known as a *'Board as a Service'* (BaaS), eliminates the needed efforts and startup costs associated with building or rebuilding a Board. As the creator of the BaaS engagement model, an industry I am credited with inventing, I can vouch for its effectiveness and viability. Due to the fact that a correctly constructed BaaS follows the structures and principles mentioned in this book for a properly architected Board, organizations can reap the benefits instantly. Be ready to be off and running day-one if you choose this option. For more on BaaS, visit http://www.integralbg.com/

Societal trends have also changed the historically insulated Board Director world through the once taboo world of individual Board Director marketing. This can also be leveraged in your Board Member candidate searches.

The Once Taboo World of Board Director Marketing

For many outside the industry, the simple term *'Board of Directors'* conjures up thoughts of dimly lit conference rooms, wafting cigar smoke and discussions of Director's escapades, not even remotely representing business situations. As entertaining as these thoughts may be, this is far from today's reality of the operations and expectations of Board accountability in the public, private, and nonprofit sectors. Today's Boards, and Board Members, have multiple additional pressures to which the scale could not have been predicted even 15 years ago - to name a few; regulation, technology advances, cybersecurity, activism, market change acceleration, and globalization have all played a role in these paradigm shifts..., but capable Board Directors and Board Advisors have indeed proactively established themselves in an industry of changing roles, increased responsibilities, and deeper demand for Board discipline. The individual and formal marketing of these Board skill sets has drastically changed.. and it all happened in an extremely short amount of time.

> ### *"The old-school approaches to Board Director marketing may no longer tell the full story"*

Most industries adopt new marketing and technology trends immediately at their introduction in their incessant race for market share. The major societal trends of social media, content & inbound marketing, and also influencer marketing, are proof of the success and relevance of these approaches for most industries. However, the Board Directorship vertical as a whole was slow to adopt these approaches in what was seen by many as a stigma in the stuffier Board field. Now, this gap has increasingly been filled by many individuals standing out in this vertical. The fact is, with the prevalence of readily available data today, you might as well control your own content. And with that belief, the flood gates have opened for Board Directors and Board Advisors to showcase their talents.

Agreed that for public company Board candidates, the actual placement is still typically done through Board search and placement companies, but what is different is that both public and private Board Directors have adopted a much different individual stance on how to simultaneously propagate their name within the industry – which can include a creative marketing strategy coupled with intriguing and informative content campaigns. Essentially *'teaching'* what they know in the covert *'sale'* of their Board expertise and experience. Ross Lauder, Chief Revenue Officer at Get Focused, states, *"Today there has been a significant paradigm shift in the way Board leadership is sought out and validated through what is considered inbound self-marketing. Self-promotion at the Board level is no longer vanity, in some cases it's expected. Traditionally, the country club locker room and old boys network were the main way connections were made in this industry... now the locker room is global and it opens the door to more diverse opportunity."*

The world of Board Director marketing is quickly catching up with the information age in its usage of once taboo marketing mechanisms

"How people market themselves for Board roles has been significantly impacted by technology," states Alyssa Gelbard, Founder & President of Point Road Group. *"Personal branding and marketing is the new normal, especially online, because it's accessible and easy. It gives a competitive advantage in this global economy by increasing visibility, which is essential since you now have to do more to be considered for coveted Board seats. While in-person presence is still vital, your LinkedIn profile, website bio, published articles, shared content, presence on social media, etc. all allow for you to be top-of-mind. It's now crucial to curate your online presence to support your Board expertise and aspirations."*

In the past, those with high skill in the Board Director industry, but afloat in shallow networking pools, never made it to most candidate piles for Board consideration. Today, a savvy Board Director, Board Advisor or Board candidate can further develop a global name for themselves through a creative marketing strategy coupled with intriguing and informative content. Do not underestimate the possibility of identifying and approaching Board candidates that leverage this approach – they should be easy to find and are likely advanced in modern communication, marketing, and sales principles based on their digital *'branding'* approach.

Board Pitch Book

Representing your Board's *'brand,'* through the practice of creating a *'Board Pitch Book,'* is invaluable in the process of attracting excellent Board Directors to your organization. A Board Pitch

Book is a formal document or presentation that lays out the fundamentals of your Board – and typically creates a Board candidate's first impression of a to-be-built Board or in-place, existing Board of Directors. A properly constructed Pitch Book creates a formal channel for introducing your Board's architecture and processes to potential candidates, and can be leveraged by private, public, and nonprofit organizations alike.

A great format for your Board Pitch Book includes many of the principles outlined in this book - and their inclusion shows a potential Board candidate the seriousness and wide-ranging future possibilities of your Board. Always consider the following areas for your Board Pitch Book:

- Company Values, Vision & Mission
- Company Credo
- Company industry and more specifically, industry vertical
- Company differentiators (in-place or planned)
- Strategy & Governance considerations
- Current company Phase of Growth
- Sphere of Influence model (including where the potential Board candidate fits)
- Planes of Congruence model (including where the potential Board candidate fits)
- Board Coverage and Balance (including where the potential Board candidate fits)
- Board Committee Structure for current phase of growth (including where the potential Board candidate fits)
- Expectations of Board Member time commitment and yearly schedule outline (more on this in Chapter 13: *'Board Member Evaluation & Selection'*

- High-level view of company financials and trending
- How the Board structure will support overall Board and individual Board Member success
- Board Member / Board Advisor compensation model
- Insurance coverage for the Board and Board Members (more on this topic in Chapter 14: *'Board Assessments, Tools and Insurance'*)
- Onboarding process and expectations

Initiate your Board Pitch Book with your company's Values, Vision & Mission. To restate an important concept from Chapter 7: *'Evaluating Values, Vision & Mission,'* I have found that effective and viable Board Members are attracted to companies with meaningful values, a strong vision statement and a resonating mission statement...[32] and once a candidate is in place on the Board, these same Board Members become the guides and governance leaders of these important facets of all companies.

It is also valuable to show both positive and negative company attributes at their current stage in the Board Pitch Book. Yes, the positive attributes will most definitely resonate with potential Board Member candidates, but many Board candidates will also be attracted to companies facing challenges or experiencing somewhat negative results, thus allowing them to apply their expertise to achieve a sense of accomplishment. Additionally, the early honesty and transparency will be greatly appreciated.

In your search, know that the quest for experienced and effective leadership is getting harder... and it is not only the executive search and placement companies taking notice. Companies of all sizes are increasingly finding it difficult to successfully fill their vacant Board and C-Level positions. The *'officer-ready'* talent pool is evaporating.

There are many reasons for this accelerating talent gap, including the shunning of formal corporate structure by the younger generations, as well as the extremely large generational population gap between the Baby Boomers and Generation X.[33] Baby Boomers are typically counted at 76 million while Generation X is accepted at a count of roughly 52-54 million. (Millennials are currently counted at roughly 75.4 million.) Add to this population gap between the Baby Boomers and Generation X the currently accelerating retirement of the Baby Boomers and you have an increasing vacuum of talent at many levels - especially noticeable at the executive and Board level. I wrote about this accelerating trend years ago in the article, *'Boards and the Baby Boomer Retirement Effect,'* where it could be strongly argued that *"not enough strategic consideration has been given to the significant business leadership experience, expertise and clout that will exit U.S. business organizations, and their Boards, during [a] relatively short retirement transition."*[34] The implications are massive. This topic is a personal favorite of mine due to the fact that when it comes to *'architecting'* Boards, the extremely dynamic and often overlooked aspect of succession planning is a topic requiring coaxing along with diplomacy. It also offers significant opportunities for Board candidates looking to further their Board Director careers.

Public companies, typically due to their status and overall limited available Board seats, are in most cases coveted Board positions. Competition can be fierce in these arenas with a high number of applicants when opened to a larger search and placement process. These statistics further support the need for structured vetting approaches and processes to quickly and effectively target the ideal candidates, even when utilizing an executive, or Board placement, firm.

Private companies, as well as most nonprofits, can experience increased challenges in attracting experienced Board Directors. Compensation, status of company, potentially increased reputational risk, and a host of other factors play integral roles in this challenge. This should not deter you, however, to approach the best candidates, even if you believe they are out of your league. I have personally witnessed properly constructed Board Pitch Books attract some of the most successful Board Directors to private companies, even when these Board Directors are primarily known for only serving on public Boards.

Whether you are part of a public, private, or nonprofit Board, put the effort into your Board Pitch Book and don't be fearful of approaching highly skilled individuals directly. You may be surprised by their response. Even if the answer is no, they will definitely remember you in a highly positive light simply based on your efforts and approach. You will hear from them again – the Board circle is very small and relational.

Board Director Age Fact: According to a study published in 2017, Fewer than 2% of S&P 500 Boards had average ages of more than 70 or less than 55.[34a]

13 BOARD MEMBER
EVALUATION & SELECTION

"Let me never fall into the vulgar mistake of dreaming that I am persecuted whenever I am contradicted."

- Ralph Waldo Emerson

"I recently approached a few people to join the board in my company..." This is a comment I hear countless times over the course of any given month in my travels and speaking engagements. On one hand, this makes me happy that more private business owners are making the leap into deeper strategy and governance for their businesses. Clearly, this is a noble endeavor. On the other hand, I am typically fearful to ask my usual follow-up questions to size-up the '*discipline*' being put into the Board build exercises. Same goes for public and nonprofit organizations. Are potential candidates simply being approached because of their success in the past, or because they have a certain level of experience? As you now know from previous chapters in this book, there is much more to this formula and process...

Remember, building or rebuilding a Board for your company is not a task, but a discipline. The most important outcome? Getting the best and most qualified people seated for the needed roles and responsibilities on your Board. So, where do you start in your Board Director evaluations and vetting? I have found over the years that my path of researching a candidate, or questions asked in interviews I conduct, including for Board candidates, follows the same successful pattern. Aptly called the '*Career Trifecta*,' this line of probing truly leads us both, interviewer and interviewee, on an interesting journey that quickly gets to the core of the candidate.

Figure 42: The Career Trifecta[35]

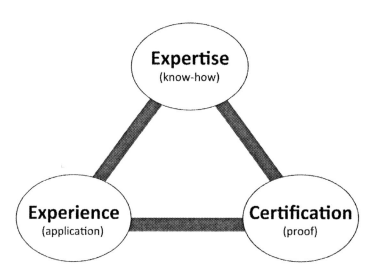

The journey first starts with understanding a Board Member's or Board candidate's level of Expertise (know-how), which equates to their level of knowledge, and the theory behind that knowledge. You want to get a feeling of how they think, some of it aligning to common industry practices, some of it bringing to the table new or interesting approaches to explore. This thought leadership attribute is very important.

As valuable as Expertise can be, it, of course, only tells a portion of the story. Graduate next to questions that put a spotlight on how those Expertise areas have been applied - which illuminates their Experience (application of knowledge). You want to get a feeling for their ability to do something well, see how they have applied their Expertise, and made a difference through their Experience. Remember that there are plenty of Board Members and Board candidates with high Expertise and skill, but not a lot of Experience, which from a Board Member standpoint can be debilitating.

The final area, to close the loop of understanding, within the Career Trifecta is the Board Member's or Board candidate's Certifications, or proof, of their Expertise and Experience.

The topic of Certification (proof) in the Board space sometimes elicits puzzled looks that either questions my comment or shows disagreement. I understand this reaction, but I have a reason for making my statement - and it can be a key differentiator when it comes to Board Members and Board candidates in all levels of their career, especially in the Board space. Old-school Board thinking is that Expertise (know-how) and Experience (application) sit alone and at the top of the mountain when it comes to Board Member ability and effectiveness. Yes, Expertise and Experience are very important, but again, the importance of these areas should be equally weighted across all three areas of the Career Trifecta.

Certification (proof) is not just a way of understanding someone's formal knowledge and training as it applies to an industry and vertical, but, possibly more importantly, a way to size-up the dedication and drive that a Board Director, or Board candidate has to the Board discipline. A serious Board Member wants as many opportunities as possible to show that Board Directorship is their career, their passion, and their discipline. Not a part-time, fleeting experiment to *see how it goes* (incidentally, *seeing how it goes'* = damage to your company). Clinton Allen, the Founder and President of The American College of Corporate Directors (ACCD), states, *"For Director candidates, and sitting public company Directors, professional Director credentials are important in demonstrating that certified Directors have taken the time and made the effort to best represent their shareholders."* A certification highlights that effort and thought were put into a Board Director's career. They take it seriously. They want to make a positive impact.

Now, before comments come back to me through email, LinkedIn, etc. on the fact that a *'certification doesn't prove everything about a candidate's worth, ethics, effectiveness, etc.'* - I get it. And I agree. I, too, know folks with some pretty high-ranking certifications that I wouldn't trust to paint a room in my house. The point is that a certification allows for another differentiator in your evaluation of great Board Directors who take their role seriously enough to invest time, effort, and money into it. Adding this as an additional decision point creates further depth in your evaluation.

Examples of Board Director certifications can be seen through The American College of Corporate Directors (ACCD) and The National Association of Corporate Directors (NACD).

Figure 43: Certification Organizations[38]

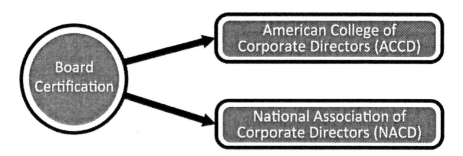

I have also found formal education courses such as Harvard Business School's Executive Education Program '*Making Corporate*

Boards More Effective,' to be quite enlightening and useful, not to mention great networking. Looking holistically at the educational angle, there are multiple certification and education paths that a Board Director can take. One isn't necessarily better than the other, but in this case, it is truly the effort that counts. Many of these certifications and educational courses cover the changing landscape of successful Board Directorship, new Board regulations, industry trending, and best practices that keep a Board Director up to speed in a quickly evolving field. This commitment to continuous learning shows a Board Director's dedication to the seriousness of their position – something for you to leverage on your Board.

Keeping in mind a quote from Chapter 9: *'Infusing Planes of Congruence in Your Board Design,'* remember that it only takes a single toxic Board member to infect the entire Board, damaging camaraderie and lowering collective Board performance. Selection criteria needs to always include unbiased and impartial evaluation processes. Allocate the needed time to do this appropriately and rigorously to ensure every Board Member is a correct fit for your Board.

Your Board will be the most important team that you construct for your business - that is why the right selection criteria is important. Above and beyond the criteria previously mentioned, it is equally important to evaluate the personality, demeanor, and leadership approach of every potential Board Member both individually, and where possible, collectively. They must be a fit in all areas. Don't settle for anything less.

In addition to the normal evaluation criteria that would be covered in standard interview processes, important additional areas of evaluation for senior levels, especially Board positions, includes the *'behavioral predisposition'* categories of IQ, EQ, MQ and TQ.

Figure 44: Behavioral Predispositions[38]

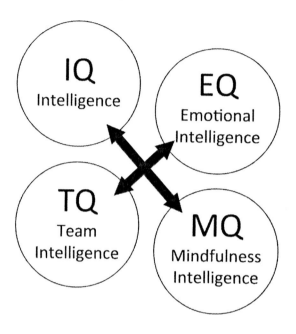

Intelligence Quotient (IQ)

The rating of an individual's overall IQ, or Intelligence Quotient, has been around since 1912, with many evolutions and enhancements since that time. However, when we are speaking about IQ in the Board Director sense, it is more an evaluation of intellectual and cognitive abilities as applied to critical thinking. Not something that can easily drawn out for evaluation during an interview, but the introduction of an example company challenge that the Board is currently facing is a great way to get a feel for how the Board candidate would step through the thought process and interact with other Board Members throughout the procedure. An actual example of a current company challenge also helps in allowing the interviewee to get involved in the deliberations, along with the interviewer, for a more authentic discussion. Additionally, there is a way to systematically evaluate and measure a Board Member or Board candidate's cognitive and critical thinking abilities through a simple online test called the Watson-Glaser Critical Thinking Appraisal (WGCTA). Although still somewhat unorthodox when it comes to *'testing'* seated Board Members or in-process Board candidates, the insight that these test results offer is incredible. The WGCTA is one of the most widely used tools for evaluating the cognitive abilities of professionals and can be a great tool to assist Boards in their evaluations. When architecting Boards, rebuilding Boards or evaluating Board candidates, this is an extremely valuable step included within my process.

Emotional Intelligence (EQ)

Emotional Quotient, typically called Emotional Intelligence, EQ, or EI, refers to *'a leader's ability to recognize, understand and manage their own emotions along with the ability to recognize, understand, and influence the emotions of others.'* EQ importantly contains the major component of empathy. Harvard Business Review's study, *'The Most Empathetic Companies, 2016,'* fortifies the importance of the empathy trait by stating, *"It is this ability to recognize and understand the emotions of others that is so important. It is also the ability to understand that our emotions have impact on others and making change as a result is more important to a successful business than it has ever been."*

The term EQ was created by two researchers, Peter Salavoy and John Mayer, and popularized in Daniel Goleman's 1996 book, *'Emotional Intelligence.'* A key point in the book was Daniel's assessment that EQ might actually be more important than IQ when considering an individual's chances of success. I write often about EQ in many of my articles due to what I believe is an uncompromisable trait for true leaders and Board Directors.

A further definition of EQ includes *'the capacity to be aware of, control, and express one's emotions, and to handle interpersonal relationships judiciously and empathetically.'* Any Board Director who views constructive feedback or criticism from fellow Board Members as an attack, or attempt to undermine their authority, needs to immediately apply some thought-leadership to their actions and responses.

Figure 45: Emotional Intelligence Domains & Competencies[36]

Self-Awareness	Self-Management	Social Awareness	Relationship Management
Emotional Self-Awareness	Emotional Self-Control	Empathy	Influence
	Adaptability		Coach & Mentor
	Achievement Orientation	Organizational Awareness	Conflict Mgmt.
			Teamwork
	Positive Outlook		Inspirational Leadership

EQ maturity is typically something that develops with time and experience, so don't expect overnight success with a Board Member or Board candidate who is not showing this trait today – and don't make the mistake of offering your boardroom as the training camp for Board candidates to hone this skill set. Existing seated Board Members with low EQ should be trained accordingly (and immediately).

The book entitled *'Emotional Intelligence 2.0'* is one outlet for informal training and should be required reading for all leaders and Board Directors. Dr. Travis Bradberry, one of the co-authors, states, *"EQ is so critical to success that it accounts for 58 percent of performance in all types of jobs. It's the single biggest predictor of performance in the workplace and the strongest driver of leadership and personal excellence."*

Similar to the Watson-Glaser Critical Thinking Inventory

(WGCTA) test mentioned for a correlation to IQ, there is also a way to systematically evaluate and measure a Board Member or Board candidate's personality characteristics for EQ evaluation - through an online test called the Gordon Personal Profile Inventory (GPP-I). The GPP-I greatly assists in discovering how a Board candidate, through what I leverage as an EQ correlation, might fit into your organization, or how a currently seated Board Member scores by assessing nine universal traits:

- Ascendance
- Responsibility
- Stress Tolerance
- Sociability
- Self Esteem
- Cautiousness
- Original Thinking
- Personal Relations
- Vigor

EQ has tremendous influence in creating an inclusive culture for a Board, as well as the company. Board dysfunction, essentially leading to poor performance, frequently manifests as an emotional disconnection caused by low EQ. When Board Members lose their 'connection' to the organization's values, mission, and to other Board Members, they are quickly consumed in a negative pattern that ultimately lowers the Board's effectiveness. High-EQ Board Members essentially eliminate meaningless emotional distractions that can consume lesser-experienced Board Directors.

With individual Board Member success, as well as overall Board success, hinging so heavily on this EQ trait, you can't afford to ignore it in your evaluation process.

Mindfulness Intelligence (MQ)

Mindfulness Quotient, typically called Mindfulness Intelligence or MQ, is the latest groundbreaking intelligence system that we'll see much more of in the near future.

Figure 45a: Mindfulness Intelligence[36a]

Mindfulness is '*the process of bringing one's attention to the internal experiences occurring in the present moment.*' In other words, are your Board Members or Board candidates looking deeper within themselves and in those around them to better understand their actions and responses. As an example, has a fellow Board Member started to exhibit performance issues? A non-mindful response would likely be for another Board Member to immediately address the issues by quickly telling them that it has to improve. On the other hand, a mindful response from a Board Member would initially include internal thoughts and questions such as:

- Inwardly Facing - Have I done everything I can to help my

fellow Board Member? Has the Board provided enough inner tools and outer resources to deal with this pressure?

- Outwardly Facing - Is there something that is making this Board Director's job less fulfilling? Has there been added stress in recent times due to a responsibility change? Is there a potential personal problem at home that is causing distraction? Are they in agreement with the direction of the Board and the company?

These types of mindful thoughts lead to much more productive and effective conversations, with a much greater chance for a motivating and successful outcome. Linda Bjork, a colleague and pioneer in the MQ arena, convincingly demonstrates the correlation of MQ to leadership success in her book *'Inner Business - Training Your Mind For Leadership Success.'* While interviewing Linda for her input on the Uber debacle outlined in Chapter 7, she pointed out, *"The multiple leadership mishaps at Uber are prime examples of serious mindfulness gaps. When you lose touch with yourself and you are in a leadership position, you are essentially trying to lead without integrity, self-awareness or a healthy mindset. All these things can be learned in a systematic, science-based way. And once you start having these conversations, you will find in what capacity mindfulness intelligence should be available to the organization and demonstrated by the leadership."*

Similar to EQ, MQ maturity is also something that develops with time and experience. Once again, don't make the mistake of offering your boardroom as the training camp for Board candidates to hone this skill set. Seated Board Members with low MQ should be trained accordingly.

Team Intelligence (TQ)

For evaluation of the all-important team dynamics of existing Boards, or when replacing Board Members, there is TQ, or Team Intelligence Quotient. Pioneered by a colleague, Dr. Solange Charas, her Ph.D. research focused on new approaches to select, develop and manage passionate high-performing interdisciplinary teams, at the Board and C-suite level, to measure their impact on corporate financial performance. In *'The Handbook of Board Governance: A Comprehensive Guide For Public, Private, and Not-For-Profit Board Members,'* Dr. Charas is quoted as saying regarding her detailed research, *"TQ in the boardroom emerged as a reliable predictor of firm performance. The implications are that enhancing team intelligence in the boardroom is key to economic value creation. Organizations with high-TQ Boards consistently outperformed their competitors on profitability performance, and organizations with low-TQ Boards consistently underperformed on profitability."* Her research led to the development of new proprietary, data-based assessment tools that can identify and coach for the appropriate behavioral characteristics to include in a new or existing Board (or any team, for that matter) for optimal performance and ultimately, success. This research proved and quantified the impact of high performing teams on financial outcomes. Dr. Charas additionally states, *"There was a statistically significant relationship between TQ at the Board and C-Suite level and the quantifiable impact of EBITDA performance between 4% and 20%. That is to say that transforming a low TQ to a high TQ team has an accretive impact on EBITDA from 4% to 20% improvement in less than 1 year. This isn't just a 'nice-to-have,' but is a 'have-to-have' if you want to out-perform competitors from a financial perspective."*

Figure 46: Aligning Proper Behavioral Predispositions[38]

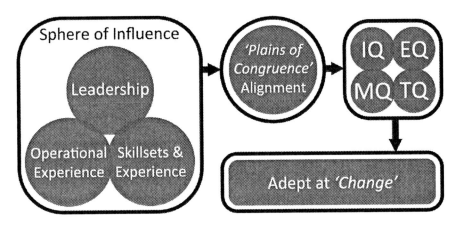

A mature balance of the mentioned behavioral predispositions is necessary for effective Board Members, and ultimately, an effective Board. After all, what good is a Board Director's experience and expertise if they don't have the diplomacy or presence to work within a team atmosphere, or read social cues from other Board Members? We have all seen the highly intelligent 'expert' that no one wants to work with. Don't do this to yourself. Don't do this to your Board. Don't do this to the company you serve. Spend the time to measure and evaluate these areas properly and leverage the mentioned available tools to assist you in evaluating successful leaders as well as team-conducive personalities. These tools and services have eliminated many false starts in my Board candidate evaluations and Board builds. They have also given incredible insight into areas that interviews simply cannot uncover.

Leveraging these evaluation categories in appointing talent is only the first hurdle. Taking proactive steps to ensure the success of recently-appointed Board Director positions is an important factor in the equation. Some studies show failure rates of new-to-role executives at 40-60%. Although there are no accurate statistics of recently-seated Board Director failures, it is logical to think that a similar, or close, correlation of percentage could be applied. These numbers demand attention. With failure rates this high, once you have decided on your perfect Board candidate and they are now in the position, you will likely want to make an effort to ensure their success. Your *'insurance policy'* can be an approach including an existing Board Member acting as an on-boarding guide or mentor, an effort that a Board can easily enact.

Front-loading your new Board Member support for the transitional and assimilation aspects can pay huge long-term rewards for not only new Board Members, but also for the overall Board.

Board Member Time Commitment

The expectation of a Board Member's time commitment to the Boards they serve is a hot topic, somewhat controversial, and has come up in just about every speaking engagement I have performed on Board topics. It is imperative that this discussion and expectation be addressed at the earliest possible time with Board Members, preferably prior to their seat appointment(s).

Why is this topic so controversial? How can their be such misalignment? Because many Board Directors underestimate the needed time to fully and successfully perform their roles. They are either not aware of the foundational Board principles covered in this book or simply want the glory of the title without committing to the effort. Others simply believe they are only present to give their *'opinions.'* Many are not viewing the responsibilities of their Board seat as a primary job, but more so as an additional hobby or secondary undertaking. This is a damaging viewpoint for the companies and organizations served by Board Members with these beliefs.

Figure 47: Yearly Board Time Commitment[38]

Title	Role / Duties	Estimated Hours
Board Director	Universal Base Duties	200
	Committee Duties (per Committee)	+50
	Board Chairperson	+50
	Committee Chair (per Committee)	+10
Board Advisor	Base Duties	50
	Committee Duties (per Committee)	+10

It is imperative that you confirm that your Board Members and Board candidates have the time to dedicate and make the commitment to their role. Reiterating from Chapter 1, *'Introduction,'* where I felt it was important to touch on this topic as early as possible, I will restate:

- I have never seen a truly successful Board Director dedicate less than 200+ hours per year per organization (public, private, or nonprofit). Supportive of this belief, a recent study by the National Association of Corporate Directors (NACD) puts the average public Board Director's yearly time commitment at 245 hours per year.[37] I believe these statistics to exactly correlate to the private and nonprofit sector, as well.

- I have never seen a truly successful Board Advisor put in less than 50 hours per year per organization (public, private, or nonprofit).

Again, this rule of thumb should be applied in public, private, and nonprofit organizations. My beliefs on this topic have likely cost me numerous Board seats over the years due to Boards that either thought that 50 or 100 hours per year per Board Member was *'adequate'* or they didn't have an opinion at all, but I am not bothered by these *'missed opportunities'* one bit. I want to be seated at the table with fellow Board Members who understand their roles, responsibilities, and what it takes to not only perform them properly, but excel. Alignment of time commitment expectation is a big factor in this formula. Don't be fearful of voicing your requirement of a high time commitment, and get this topic aligned and settled as early as possible.

I have included a recent communication on this topic following a comment I left on a post on LinkedIn where I once again mentioned, *"I have never seen a truly successful Board Director dedicate less than 200+ hours per year per organization they serve (public, private, or nonprofit)."* The response to this was, *"Thanks for your comment, Mark. In fairness to the venture community, while 200-250 hours is a good benchmark for U.S. public companies (per NACD data), I would respectfully agree with many on Sand Hill Road that it's arguably less so for many private companies (particularly startups through Series B). I advise a number of Series B boards, for example, with high caliber, fiercely proactive/independent boards, where each director spends more like 100-125 hours per year. Is that contrary to your experience?"*

(By the way, *'Sand Hill Road,'* often shortened to just *'Sand Hill,'* is an arterial road in Menlo Park, California, notable for its concentration of Venture Capital companies.)

No, it is not contrary to my experience with Boards in the private company and Venture Capital community, but that doesn't make it right. Yes, I still believe that a truly successful Board Director must dedicate 200+ hours per year per organization they serve (public, private, or nonprofit). Why do I still believe this even while knowing that the VC community has lived by a different standard? For the simple reason that the VC community has a laser focus on speed of growth that many times sidesteps the long-term focus on values, culture, and operations – all to get, as quickly as possible, to unicorn-like status and/or company sale. This is why I don't typically entertain Board seat invitations from

VC companies unless they have serious existing Board structure already in place or in scenarios where I have person'lly architected the Board structure. I propose a different overall approach for VC Boards in which they focus more holistically on the company for longer-term success, which inherently increases overall value, but would absolutely require more focus and time from the Board.

Avoiding Zombie Directors:

Yes, there is actually such a thing as *'Zombie Directors'*! This term is typically associated with public company Board Members who have failed to get a majority of shareholder votes in elections, but continue to serve on the Board. For private companies and nonprofit organizations, I like to expand upon this definition and think of Zombie Directors as those who don't regularly attend scheduled Board meetings (potentially due to *'overboarding'*), lack Board discipline, or have low Board expectations - all enabled by lax Board governance. When these Board Members do attend meetings, they arrive unprepared and behave *'zombie-like'* during important discussion topics and decisions.

The public company zombie phenomenon is an interesting one. In the November 7th, 2016 Washington Post article, *'The Zombie Directors Who Lurk on Corporate Boards,'* Jena McGregor addresses a study on Russell 3000 companies' zombie directors and writes, *"All of those [zombie] directors serve on Boards that have what's called a 'plurality' standard rather than a 'majority' one. In these, Boards only require that Directors receive more votes than a compelling candidate. Yet since most Directors run uncontested, they can win by getting a single vote."* Further data from Institutional Shareholder Services (ISS) shows a total of 225 scenarios from 2012 to 2016 where Board Directors of public companies got less than half the votes cast... but only 44 of those Board Directors exited the Board within the next election cycle. Following investor and activist noise on this topic, companies have been more open to agreeing to terms in which Directors who don't receive a majority of votes have to tender their resignation. This growing practice, however, isn't a foolproof solution as Boards are typically not required to accept these resignations. This opens the door for Boards to reinstate unelected Directors without any repercussions. Hence, a larger than expected public Board zombie population.

In my modified definition of Zombie Directors, as applied to private companies and nonprofit organizations, they truly can be bloodsucking and harmful to the overall health of the organization they have committed to serve. Wavering, noncommittal, and partial involvement, not to mention unpreparedness with little value-add when present, is quite detrimental to not only a company or organization, but also to the camaraderie of the Board - this lowers the entire Board to the level of its weakest player. For private companies, this can almost ensure floundering progress and negative results. For nonprofit organizations, this can be a death sentence.

Nonprofit organizations likely have the largest infestation of my alternate definition of Zombie Directors due to these organizations' historically lax candidate approval processes and frequently lacking role & responsibility governance. In any organization, it is vital to identify the zombies and banish these 'living dead' from the organization.

All of the provided structures, examples, and anecdotes are designed to help you work through your ideal Board candidate search and vetting processes. They can also be used to reevaluate existing seated Board Members and the overall Board. Remember that dedicated efforts initiated early on in this process can help eliminate false starts, lessen disruption, and avoid strife within your Board.

Board Candidate Fact: Organizations are awakening to the benefits of creating a Board *'mixtocracy,'* essentially infusing the positive attributes of *'meritocracy,'* while simultaneously aiming to exclude the potential risks of *'mirrortocracy.'* Consequently, Boards are increasingly exploring the inclusion of *"nontraditional members who will be balanced out by more traditional ones"* in their quest for diversity on multiple levels.[38a]

Mark A. Pfister

14 BOARD ASSESSMENTS, TOOLS, & INSURANCE

"The difficulty lies not in the new ideas, but in escaping from the old ones."

- John Maynard Keynes

Board Assessments

Once you have architected and built your ideal Board, you have a vested interest in protecting what has been created. All Boards require attention and *'maintenance'* to keep them operating at an exceptional level. In addition to yearly Board architectural and structural reviews (identified through the processes outlined in this book), formal evaluations of the entire Board (as a team), coupled with individual Board Member evaluations set the precedent for expected performance.

Oddly, this seemingly obvious evaluation exercise is not implemented by a significant percentage of Boards. The 2016–2017 *'NACD Public Company Governance Survey'*[39] reported that only 31% of respondents viewed improving the Board evaluation process as an important, or very important, priority for their Boards over the following 12 months. In fact, just 41% of Boards participating in the survey currently use individual Board evaluations. An even smaller number of Boards use the results of these evaluations to make decisions about replacing Board Directors. Don't make this mistake with your Board. Whether a public, private, or nonprofit Board, set the expectation and follow-though on performing meaningful and actionable yearly reviews.

The process of performing these reviews can range from informal to extremely detailed, but know that serious efforts put into this exercise aids in setting the tone for your organization, and also the seriousness of a Board Member's responsibility. Ernst & Young's Center for Board Matters created an excellent guide entitled *'Accelerating Board Performance: The Importance of Assessments'*[40] for this purpose. This document is intended to *"provide Boards with useful tools, tips, and considerations for increasing Board effectiveness through an enhanced approach to Board assessments,"*[40] with sections covering:

- *'Board Assessments: A strategic opportunity in a complex environment'*

- *'Balancing It All: Managing multiple priorities and stakeholders'*

- *'Key Elements of Board Effectiveness: What to assess'*

- *'Different Approaches: Finding the right way to assess your Board'*

- *'The Importance of Board Dynamics: Working cohesively as a team'*

- *'After The Board Assessment: Making plans for positive change'*

- *'Example Board Evaluation'*

For public companies in the U.S., the NYSE Listing Company Manual, Section 303A.09,[41] mandates that the Board of Directors of all NYSE-listed companies *'conduct a self-evaluation at least annually to determine whether it and its committees are functioning effectively.'*[41] Private and nonprofit organizations should *'borrow'* this mandate and implement it with the same discipline required by public companies. Leverage the previously mentioned existing framework in creating a detailed roadmap for your own customized Board evaluations.

Tools

Ease of collaboration and information sharing is key for a Board to truly be successful. Many times, Board Members are not all located in the same geographical region, nor are all Board Members created equal when it comes to technical knowledge to efficiently share information. Some Boards try to overcome these challenges with additional conference calls and lengthy emails, but these mediums are typically not sufficient in creating an increasingly collaborative environment. Board Portals, secure software or websites designed to facilitate communication and to act as a central repository aiding in presenting, reviewing, commenting, and voting, are great tools to bridge this gap. Today's Board Portals have come a long way in allowing for the sharing, capture, and dissemination of information prior, during, and between Board meetings.

Boards, depending on their composition, have varying needs and requirements when it comes to simplifying and fostering collaboration. What is consistent, however, are recurring elements that seem to be persistent challenges for a majority of Boards to streamline. These include:

- Board Book Creation: A Board Book, designed to provide an integrated and consolidated view of an upcoming

Board Meeting's agenda and content in advance of a Board Meeting, is an important component of preparation and review for all Board Members. It also serves as the formal outline and guide to keep a Board Meeting on track. Board Portals allow for not only increased structure and efficiency in this process, but also a consistent format to promote full Board Book content review by Board Members in advance of all Board meetings.

- Sharing and Accessing Documents: A secure document repository with ease of sharing is helpful for any organization, but essential to create a well-organized Board. Board Portals allow for current documentation, as well as archived documentation, to be easily posted, searched, and referenced.

- Calendar Sharing & Scheduling: Needless to say, Board Directors are typically very busy individuals. Coordinating of calendars for interim meetings, Board Committee meetings, Board meetings, etc. are not always an easy task. Unfortunately, the complexity of this task increases exponentially with the size of a Board. Board Portals containing a calendar module can greatly streamline coordination efforts without the need for countless emails, requests, and reminders.

- Board Committee Collaboration: Even when a Board's formal Board meeting documentation is up to par, a common area that frequently lacks structure is documentation relating to Board Committee work. Remembering that the bulk of a Board's work is completed within the Board Committees, this trend can be debilitating and hinder progress. Great Board Portals have *'workspaces'* dedicated to Board Committees with a mechanism to attach or post documentation for frequent dissemination and to ease incorporation into the Board Book.

The wish for Board Portals to contain integrated video-conferencing and presentation tools for remote Board Members needs to be addressed, however. While researching this coveted communication component for this book, a few of the well-known names in the Board Portal space acknowledged the need, the common request, and the fact that this was a priority in their development. From my standpoint, this is by no means an acceptance of remote Board meetings in place of in-person Board meetings, but the necessity for inclusive tools when the need arises should be addressed.

Identifying, investigating, and selecting the best Board Portal solution is a perfect instance to enact a special project to define which one meets your specific Board's needs.

Insuring The Board

An often discussed, but frequently misunderstood, insurance product integral to a Board's welfare is Director & Officer insurance, commonly referred to as D&O insurance.

D&O insurance, by definition, is liability insurance *'payable to the Directors and Officers of a company, or to the organization itself, as indemnification (reimbursement) for losses or advancement of defense costs in the event an insured suffers such a loss as a result of a legal action brought for alleged wrongful acts in their capacity as Directors and Officers. Such coverage can extend to defense costs arising out of criminal and regulatory investigations/trials as well; in fact, often civil and criminal actions are brought against Directors/Officers simultaneously. It has become closely associated with broader management liability insurance, which covers liabilities of the corporation itself as well as the personal liabilities for the Directors and*

Officers of the corporation. Intentional illegal acts, however, are typically not covered under D&O policies.'[42]

Although the Business Judgment Rule, a legal presumption *'that in making a business decision, the Directors of a corporation acted on an informed basis, in good faith and in the honest belief that the action taken was in the best interests of the company,'[44]* is still alive and well, it is an overall assumption that cannot cover certain specific legal claims requiring deeper investigation.

D&O insurance was first marketed in the 1930s, but didn't get deeper traction until the 1960s. Similar to the history of governance (Chapter 6: *'The Role of Governance'*), D&O insurance was popularized in the U.S. during the rapid growth of merger & acquisition (M&A) activities. Numerous and costly litigations in the M&A arena during a relatively short time period greatly increased costs in the form of premiums and reduced availability. This also forced much of the complicated language and exclusionary clauses incorporated in D&O coverage to this day.

Historically, D&O insurance has been overwhelmingly associated with large, multi-national public corporations' Boards and Officers, however, trending shows increasing adoption with companies and organizations outside the public realm. Savvy Board Directors of any organization type know that they are increasingly at risk for lawsuits and claims filed against the companies they serve. Stakeholders can attempt to hold Boards, and even individual Board Members, of any organization type liable for financial losses or other negative consequences experienced by their respective organizations... and, regardless of a Board Director's culpability, may encounter a need to properly represent themselves legally no matter how prudently they acted. This scenario would no doubt be a costly undertaking to take on personally. Hence, the growing desire for private and nonprofit Board Directors, alongside public Board Directors, to require D&O

insurance before agreeing to join any Board as a voting Board Member.

According to the Allianz Global Corporate & Specialty *'Introduction to D&O Insurance'* Risk Briefing,[43] very specific areas are covered and not covered by standard D&O policies:

Covered (by example of *'common D&O risk scenarios'*): [43]

- *'Employment practices & HR issues'*
- *'Shareholder actions'*
- *'Reporting errors'*
- *'Inaccurate or inadequate disclosure (e.g. in company accounts)'*
- *'Misrepresentation in a prospectus'*
- *'Decisions exceeding the authority granted to a company officer'*
- *'Failure to comply with regulations or laws'*

Not Covered (by example of *'common D&O exclusions'*):[43]

- *'Fraud'*
- *'Intentional non-compliant acts'*
- *'Illegal remuneration or personal profit'*
- *'Property damage and bodily harm (except Corporate Manslaughter)'*
- *'Legal action already taken when the policy begins'*
- *'Claims made under a previous policy'*
- *'Claims covered by other insurance'*

As a simple rule of thumb for a Board Director, *'if you have a vote, you should have D&O.'* The personal risk is becoming increasingly too great to take a chance otherwise. Board Advisors, and subsequently a Board of Advisors, having no voting ability, do not require D&O - a common Error & Omission insurance (E&O) policy typically will suffice in these scenarios.

It should be noted that D&O insurance has a reputation for its high base cost with a common need, depending on risk tolerance, for adding additional expensive coverage 'modules.' There are no feasible and safe workarounds for not offering this coverage in public companies and nonprofit organizations, however, there exists an interim option for private companies when architecting a new Board build – initiating the Board as a Board of Advisors for an agreed timeline and then graduating members to full Board Member status after a predefined, and evaluated, period. As long as you form the Board as a Board of Advisors (non-voting with no fiduciary responsibilities), D&O insurance is not required. Incentives for this 'graduating' model can be in the form of vested equity to be offered at the time of transition from Board Advisor to Board Member in return for previous service (note that at the point of changing from a Board of Advisors to a Board of Directors, D&O insurance would then be required). Remember, this entire compensation model should be included in your Board Pitch Book.

⇒ For further detail on overall non-employee Board Member compensation within public companies, see the annual 'Director Compensation Report' by Pearl Meyer.[45] This is a great resource for understanding base pay percentages by company size and also overall compensation package makeup – it can also be utilized as a baseline when formulating private company Board Member pay and/or compensation packages. Pearl Meyer collaborates with the National Association of Corporate Directors (NACD) to publish its annual Director Compensation Report based upon the analysis of the disclosures of 1,400 public companies across 24 industries.

In addition to covering your Board and its members with proper legal indemnifications, the insurance topic can be a major factor in attracting and retaining great Board Members. There are countless cases of savvy Board Directors turning down Board seats due to nonexistent D&O insurance, or D&O coverage that is not sufficient to properly protect against common potential legal risks. If you have existing D&O insurance for your Board already in place, build a process to perform a yearly review that reevaluates its suitability for your company and Board's current state and phase of growth. If you are in the early stages of building your Board for a private company, remember that insurance coverage, or future coverage plans, is a great topic to include in your Board Pitch Book for potential Board candidates.

Board Assessment Fact: When implemented through a formal process, Board evaluations are a great tool to reinforce appropriate Board roles. They also serve to bring out inherent issues and challenges that aren't spoken about openly - all in an effort to properly solution them. Evaluations provide the board *"an opportunity to identify and remove obstacles to better perforn·mce and to highlight best practices,"* essentially elevating the entire organization.[46]

Mark A. Pfister

15 IMPLEMENTATION
SUMMARY & MOTIVATION

"Whosoever desires constant success must change [their] conduct with the times"

- Niccolò Machiavelli

This book has dedicated the majority of Board architecture teachings and examples to *proactive* approaches to aid in your roadmap of building or rebuilding your Board. I would be remiss to close without addressing preparedness for instances requiring *reactive* Board response. As a rule of thumb, Boards should equally dedicate time to proactive as well as reactive preparedness. Creating mock *'what if'* scenarios may seem like a waste of time, but these are very simple exercises that can be undertaken to practice strategic and well-orchestrated crisis responses. An increasing percentage of Boards now receive consistent reports containing not only top risks currently facing their organization, but also summaries of emerging risks internal and external to their overall industry as a way of staying more widely informed on potential reactive scenarios. This is a great Board practice to abide by and will most definitely save precious time if and when a reactive situation is encountered.

Reactive Board Preparedness

Let's expand on this reactive preparation approach through an interesting, yet unexpected, example relating to a PR crisis instance. I will start by admitting that I am not a big TV watcher, however, during a dinner meeting conversation, a popular TV episode was being discussed. A dinner guest referenced the show 'This Is Us,' specifically the episode that aired following the 2018 Super Bowl. The dinner conversation was interesting enough to make me watch the episode a few days later – but not for the need of drama or to get hooked on a TV series, but more so to specifically see a scene in which I was told a Crock-Pot slow cooker, given to the father, Jack Pearson (Milo Ventimiglia), by a neighbor, ignites a fire that burns down the home. Jack, a beloved character on the show, is killed.

Now, it is safe to say that most folks would want to see the fire scene simply for the suspense, camera work and final outcome. Not me. The only thing that I could think of was, "...*what company owns Crock-Pot and what a PR nightmare for them! I wonder what their Board was doing right at that moment?*"

The next day, I decided to do some research on the company's response – and I was both shocked and impressed by the chain of events.

Turns out, approximately 27 million people tuned in to watch the 'This Is Us' episode following the Super Bowl. This level of viewership was incredible for the show, but absolutely terrible for Newell Brands, the makers of Crock-Pot. It should be mentioned that although the term and brand 'Crock-Pot' was not directly mentioned in the episode, such a kitchen legend required no introduction – and it subsequently became an instant victim of its own success. During the episode's airing, and continuing after the end of the episode, thousands of fans of the show voiced their dismay on Twitter regarding Jack's death... and also their intent (and request of others) to throw out their Crock-Pots!

This turned into an instantaneous and national outcry against Crock-Pot, igniting in less than 30 seconds – all following a fictitious and scripted scene that had nothing to do with any actual actions of Newell Brands. A seemingly harmless scene on a popular TV show plunged Newell Brands into an immediate and full-fledged PR crisis.

Newell Brands, as if on cue, immediately took to social media, created the Twitter account @CrockPotCares, and posted a thoughtful and compassionate response:

"THIS IS US SPOILER ALERT. We're still trying to mend our heart after watching This Is Us on Tuesday night. America's favorite dad and husband deserved a better exit and Crock-Pot shares in your devastation. Don't further add to this tragedy by throwing your Crock-Pot Slow Cooker away. It's hard to pass something down from generation to generation if you throw it away (grandma won't be too happy). Spending time with his family while enjoying comfort food from his Crock-Pot was one of his favorite things to do. Let's all do our part and honor his legacy in the kitchen with Crock-Pot."

In addition to social media channels, Newell Brands quickly engaged mainstream media with the following statement:

"For nearly 50 years, with over 100 million Crock-Pots sold, we have never received any consumer complaints similar to the fictional events portrayed in last night's episode. In fact, the safety and design ⟨f our product renders this type of event nearly impossible.

In addition, and most relevant to the concerns consumers are having after watching the recent This Is Us episode, our Crock-Pot slow cookers are low current, low wattage (typically no more than 200 or 300 watts) appliances with self-regulating heating elements."

A week later, Newell Brands was still at it with supportive messages, showing empathy towards fans of the show, and also injecting a little humor with the hashtag, *#CrockPotIsInnocent*.

Newell Brand's Board likely never saw this type of exposure coming from a seemingly unrelated TV scene. In fairness, how could any company or Board prepare for an *'instance'* such as this? Truth is, they can't. However, what companies and Boards can absolutely do is be prepared for a *'scenario'* such as this. Practicing *'what if'* scenarios relating to potential crises are key. Although not verified, I would like to believe after witnessing a flawless crisis response, Newell Brands' Board was most definitely prepared for this type of *'scenario.'*

Strategic Systematic Thought Process

There is a final concept I would like to share in an effort to assist with a Board Director's, and the overall Board's, effectiveness and sustainability. This is a simple strategic systematic thought process that serves Board Members well. The concept was quickly referenced in Chapter 11: *'The Importance of Board Committees,'* when discussing Board Committee Processes and Procedures, and it is worth elaborating and expanding upon for overall Board process adoption.

Figure 48: Systematic Strategic Thought Process[38]

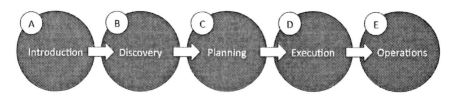

By initially classifying, or compartmentalizing, every idea, concept, strategy, challenge, etc. introduced to the Board into the following *'phases,'* it allows for a defined starting point of deliberation for all parties involved:

- Introduction

- Discovery

- Planning

- Execution

- Operations (meaning fully launched and operational)

This thought process can be leveraged by a Board in many ways, most importantly in the following two:

- Internal to the Board: All initiatives undertaken by the Board, or Board Committees, can design their step-by-step process to follow these phases, offering clear and transparent insight into their approach and progress – as milestones. This is also a great reporting methodology to align a consistent reporting format across the Board and Board Committees.

- External to the Board: Ideas, concepts, strategies, challenges, etc. introduced to the Board can be quickly *'sized-up'* on current state and status, who is or should be involved, and, if applicable, which previous phase(s) failed in their approach or implementation requiring further investigation.

There is an inherent challenge faced by groups and teams, including Boards, to quickly get to a baseline discussion starting point. With a systematic strategic thought process instituted by a Board, the initial goal becomes to prioritize the leveling of an '*entry point*' so that everyone is quickly starting from the same vantage point. For Boards, time is always of the essence, and getting the Board to a common launch point quickly is imperative. This concept is not suggesting an assimilation of viewpoints by any means, but more so a quick and systematic approach to get to a leveled starting point for discussion and deliberation. I, along with Board Directors I coach and mentor, consistently apply this strategic thought process in Board operations to ensure successful outcomes in a timely manner.

A further expansion of this systematic strategic thought process can also be very useful in support of a Board's '*noses in, fingers out*' approach when planning or evaluating their actions. This viewpoint of compartmentalizing the actual phases into a strategic vs. tactical comparison greatly helps in the decisioning of where a Board should or should not be involved - or '*how*' they should be involved. Today's Boards are overseeing an exponential amount of information and challenges, so a systematic approach to quickly categorizing what is the responsibility of the Board and what is the responsibility of management can greatly assist in eliminating Board paralysis.

Figure 49: Expanded Systematic Strategic Thought Process[38]

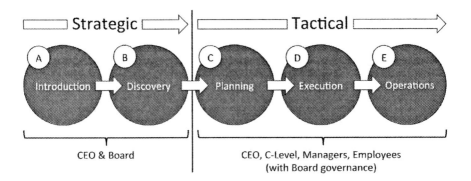

<table>
<thead>
<tr><th>CEO & Board</th><th>CEO, C-Level, Managers, Employees (with Board governance)</th></tr>
</thead>
</table>

Yes, there are certain situations where a fine delineation between strategic/tactical and Board/management cannot be drawn, but most common Board occurrences can easily be categorized for immediate reflection. Leveraging this proven practice can increase efficiency and effectiveness within your Board.

Summary

In fulfilling our journey together, know that there is much effort and work to architect and implement your Board properly. This is also true in keeping your Board at a high-performing level through innovative strategies, effective governance, and ongoing improvement. Never stop learning and never stop improving. The outcome is worth it. As Teddy Roosevelt famously stated, *"Nothing in the world is worth having or worth doing unless it means effort, pain, difficulty..."*

I truly hope you have enjoyed this book and have found the information and recommendations useful, as well as implementable in your environment. It was a pleasure to share these proven methodologies with you. Remember, when creating and implementing effective Board architecture, it is an ongoing journey, not necessarily a finite destination. Leverage and reference this book frequently as your roadmap and guide... and always have a strategy coupled with aligned governance. In summary of our journey together:

- Be extremely clear on your reasoning to build a Board, or why you want to rebuild an existing Board,

- Remember what makes a great Board, along with the traits of great Board Members,

- Fully understand the role and absolute importance of Strategy and Governance,

- Be sure to evaluate, and possibly update or revamp, your company's Values, Vision, Mission, and Credo,

- Spend the needed time and thought-leadership on creating your Board's foundational Sphere of Influence and Planes of Congruence,

- Build a simple mechanism to understand and track your Board Member Coverage & Balance,

- Do the proper due-diligence to construct your Board Committees with extreme care due to the inherent importance they wield on your Board's (and company's) ongoing success,

- Whether you are looking for a single Board Member or an entire Board, construct an outstanding Board Pitch Book to properly convey your Board's architecture strategy, path of trajectory, and prowess,

- Utilize multiple channels, including formal and informal, to find and attract the best Board candidates,

- Remain extremely discerning during your Board Member Evaluation & Selection process, and always ensure both leadership and operations expertise,

- Fully understand the options and motivational principles behind Board Member compensation options,

- Create a continually-improving Board environment through formal and consistent Board, and Board Member, assessments,

- Know how to protect your Board, the organization, and yourself with proper D&O insurance and coverage,

- Leverage modern Board tools, such as Board Portal software or websites, to streamline your governance and information sharing,

- Instill in your Board environment a Systematic Strategic Thought Process that allows all Board Members to quickly get on the same page and level prior to engaging in deliberations, and finally,

- Know that architecting a great Board of Directors or Board of Advisors takes time, focus, and work. Treat it as a formal project with phases and milestones. The outcome is worth it.

Wishing you all great success and fulfillment in your Board endeavors. Reach out to let me know of your challenges, as well as your triumphs.

Onward and upward,

Mark A. Pfister
www.PfisterStrategy.com

> *"Don't fear failure so much that you refuse to try new things. The saddest summary of a life contains three descriptions: could have, might have, and should have.."*
>
> - Louis E. Boone

For assistance with your Board, Executive Leadership and Management Consulting initiatives, visit:

www.PfisterStrategy.com

National Speaking Tours

- Building an Effective Board For Your Company
- Becoming an Exceptional Board Director Candidate
- The Strategy of Strategy
- (Check website for additional upcoming tours)

Independent/Outside Board Director

- Available for select Board Director & Board Advisor Positions

Consulting

- Board Build – Strategic Planning & Structuring Engagement
- Board Evaluation – Strategic Review & Expert Advisory
- Company Growth Advisory Services
- The Strategy Workshop
- Becoming an Exceptional Board Director Candidate Course
- Expert Program / Project Management
- The Entrepreneur Course: 10 Easy Steps to Start Your Own Business (online & on-demand course)

Newsletter

Sign up for my semi-monthly *'Across The Board'* newsletter publication - a Board Director, Board Advisor, and Business Newsletter reaching 24,000+ thought-leaders and visionaries in over 65 countries with articles focused on leadership, strategy, and governance topics – www.PfisterStrategy.com

LinkedIn

Connect with me on LinkedIn at:
www.linkedin.com/in/markapfister/

MARK A. PFISTER
BIOGRAPHY

Mark A. Pfister is CEO of M. A. Pfister Strategy Group, an executive management firm that serves as a strategic advisory council for executives and Boards in the private, public, and nonprofit sectors. He is also CEO of Integral Board Group and the Chairman of the Board. He is a *'Board Macro-Influencer'* and his success has been repeated across a wide range of business situations and environments. Mr. Pfister prides himself on being a coach and mentor to senior executives and is sought by teammates for his unique skill sets. In Board Director circles, Mr. Pfister has earned the nickname, *'The Board Architect.'*

The overarching theme throughout Mr. Pfister's career has been his aptitude in leadership positions, passionate focus on people, unique governance models, and also his ability to create value for shareholders and stakeholders through innovative business strategies and operational excellence. Michael Lorelli, the Executive Chairman of Rita's Franchise Company, has said, *"Mark's unusual combination of excelling at a macro and micro grasp of business, genuine interest in Governance and ability to coach and mentor a Management Team make him a terrific Independent Director."*

Mr. Pfister is a certified Expert Project Manager and frequently consults on global projects and programs in their initiation phases as well as programs that require remedial focus to bring them back on track. He has deep knowledge and experience in entrepreneurship, turnaround management, succession planning, data analytics, and consults companies of all sizes in business strategy, structure, development, operations, and raising capital.

Prior to forming M. A. Pfister Strategy Group and joining Integral Board Group, Mr. Pfister was CEO of Pro4ia, Inc., a national consulting and professional services company specializing in a wide range of technology solutions utilizing formal Project Management as a proven and repeatable delivery method. Pro4ia was Citibank's Nominee for Crain's Magazine *'Entrepreneurship of the Year'* Award in 2005. He simultaneously served as CEO of Onit, Inc., a national sourcing company with innovative compensation models, specializing in placements for all levels of technology skill sets within support environments.

Previously, Mr. Pfister was the National Program Office leader for American Express driving strategic projects within their technology group. Mr. Pfister served as a Licensed Engineering Officer in the U.S. Merchant Marine, holds a B.S. from the State University of New York Maritime College in Facilities Engineering and completed Harvard Business School's Executive Education Program for Board Directors.

Mr. Pfister is considered to be the creator of the *'Board as a Service'* (BaaS) engagement model, an industry he is credited with inventing, and frequently lectures on this topic. He is a master speaker and conducts national speaking engagements, lectures, courses, and seminars focused on effective leadership, strategy, Board architecture, Board candidacy, professional project/program management and entrepreneurship.

Mr. Pfister is an exceptional CEO and Board of Directors candidate for public or private companies. He is typically the Chair or a member of the Strategic Planning Committee, Technology & Cybersecurity Committee, Compensation Committee and Governance Committee. He also consults as a Board Advisor and Executive Coach to multiple public company Committee Chairs and Board Members.

He is a Certified Board Director through the American College of Corporate Directors (ACCD), a member of the National Association of Corporate Directors (NACD), a certified Project Management Professional (PMP) through the Project Management Institute (PMI) and holds a Certified Cyber Intelligence Professional (CCIP) Board Certification through the McAfee Institute.

www.PfisterStrategy.com

NOTES & QUOTES

Chapter 1:

- 1: Figure 1 & Figure 2 – Introduction section from 2017/2018 National Speaking Tour: *'Building an Effective Board For Your Company'* by Mark A. Pfister

- 2: 2015 Survey on Board of Directors of Nonprofit Organizations by David F. Larcker, Nicholas E. Donatiello, Bill Meehan, Brian Tayan. Stanford GSB, Rock Center for Corporate Governance, BoardSource, and GuideStar. April 2015

- 3: *'Data in new study pinpoints major problems for nonprofit leaders'* by Marc A. Pitman, Mar 15, 2016. Nonprofit Sector Leadership Report 2016

- 3a: 2016–2017 NACD Public Company Governance Survey

- 4: Adapted from Introduction section from 2017/2018 National Speaking Tour: *'Building an Effective Board For Your Company'* by Mark A. Pfister

- 5: Spencer Stuart's published study, *'2016 Board Index of S&P 500 Companies.'*

- 6: Harvard Law School Forum on Corporate Governance and Financial Regulation, *'Declassified Boards Are More Likely To Be Diverse,'* by Grant Bremer, Equilar

- 7: Diane Posnak, Managing Director, Pearl Meyer & Partners, 2003

- 7a: Definition as defined by Investopedia

- 7b: Definition as defined by Wikipedia

- 7c: Cyril O'Donnell, Origins of the Corporate Executive, __Bull. of the Bus. Hist. Soc. 55, 61 (1952)

Chapter 2:

- 8: Adapted from Introduction section from 2017/2018 National Speaking Tour: *'Building an Effective Board For Your Company'* by Mark A. Pfister

- 9: Introduction section from 2017/2018 National Speaking Tour: *'Building an Effective Board For Your Company'* by Mark A. Pfister

- 10: Types of political authority first defined by Max Weber in his essay *'Politics as a Vocation'*

- 11: Forbes article, *'The Facts Of Family Business'* by contributor Aileron, July 31st, 2013

- 12: Article – *'The Board's Enhanced Role in Business Succession'* by Mark A. Pfister, March 6th, 2017

- 13: Lodestone Global's *'2016 Private Company Board Compensation Survey'*

Chapter 4:

- 14: Harvard Business Review – *'The New Science of Building Great Teams,'* by Alex 'Sandy' Pentland - From the April 2012 Issue

Chapter 5:

- 15: Adapted from AT Kearny: *'The History of Strategy and its Future Prospects'*

- 15a: The Board's Proposed Role in Strategy: Adapted from *'Great Boards'* 2005, Vol. V., No. 2

- 15b: *'How Big Data Wrecked Democracy Forever: A Pivot in Campaigning Strategy That Changed The World,'* by Mark A. Pfister published in May of 2017
  https://www.linkedin.com/pulse/how-big-data-wrecked-democracy-forever-mark-a-pfister/

- 15c: Business Insider, *'A Venture Capital Firm Just Named An Algorithm To Its Board Of Directors — Here's What It Actually Does'* by Rob Wile, May 13, 2014
  http://www.businessinsider.com/vital-named-to-board-2014-5

- 15d: 2016–2017 NACD Public Company Governance Survey

Chapter 6:

- 16: Word lineage as defined by Wikipedia

- 17: Adapted from Governance section from 2017/2018 National Speaking Tour: *'Building an Effective Board For Your Company'* by Mark A. Pfister

- 18: Adapted from Noam Noked, co-editor, HLS Forum

on Corporate Governance and Financial Regulation & the Deloitte Governance Framework

- 19: Adapted from Board Effect's *'Board Governance Models: A Comprehensive List'* by Jeremy Barlow

- 20: Ernst & Young: *'Younger Managers Rise in the Ranks - Members of Each Generation: Perceived Characteristics'* - http://www.ey.com/us/en/issues/talent-management/talent-survey-members-of-each-generation-perceived-characteristics

- 21: *'Championing a Multi-Generational Workforce With Visual Communication'* by Matt Pierce – https://trainingmag.com/championing-multi-generational-workforce-visual-communication

- 22: Knoll - *Generational Preferences: A Glimpse Into the Future Office* - https://www.knoll.com/knollnewsdetail/generational-preferences-a-glimpse-into-the-future-office

- 23: *'Effective Employee Training in a Multi-Generational Workforce'* - BizLibrary - Chris Osborn & Jessica Batz, January 9, 2013 - January 9, 2013 https://www.slideshare.net/BizLib/effective-employee-training-in-a-multigenerational-workforce

- 23a: Strategy+Business: Corporate Strategies and News Articles on Global Business, Management, Competition and Marketing, February 14, 2003 / Spring 2003 / Issue 30 (originally published by Booz & Company) Strategy & Leadership, *'Corporate Governance: Hard Facts about Soft Behaviors - Seven steps to fixing what Sarbanes-Oxley can't'* by Paul Kocourek, Christian Burger, and Bill Birchard

Chapter 7:

- 24: Adapted from 2017/2018 National Speaking Tour: *'Becoming an Exceptional Board Director Candidate'* by Mark A. Pfister

- 24a: Dora Wang, TINYpulse, '4 Facts You Should Know About Company Culture & Values, December 3, 2015

Chapter 8:

- 25: Adapted from 2017/2018 National Speaking Tour: *'Becoming an Exceptional Board Director Candidate'* by Mark A. Pfister

- 26: Adapted from The Journal of Nonprofit Management - *'Developing Leadership on Boards of Directors'* by Barbara Miller
  http://www.boardcoach.com/downloads/Developing-Leadership-on-Boards-Board-Leadership-Project-Governance-Matters.pdf

Chapter 9:

- 27: Adapted from 2017/2018 National Speaking Tour: *'Building an Effective Board For Your Company'* by Mark A. Pfister

- 28: Oxford Dictionary Definition of Emotional Intelligence
  https://en.oxforddictionaries.com/definition/emotional_intelligence

Chapter 11:

- 29: Wiktionary dictionary term
  https://en.wiktionary.org/wiki/a_camel_is_a_horse_designed_by_a_committee

- 30: Adapted from the Board Committee section from 2017/2018 National Speaking Tour: *'Building an Effective Board For Your Company'* by Mark A. Pfister

Chapter 12:

- 31: Adapted from the *'Ensuring Success: Available Options and Services to Build Your Board'* section from 2017/2018 National Speaking Tour: *'Building an Effective Board For Your Company'* by Mark A. Pfister

- 32: Adapted from 2017/2018 National Speaking Tour: *'Becoming an Exceptional Board Director Candidate'* by Mark A. Pfister

- 33: November 9, 2017 Across The Board newsletter publication: *'The Evaporating Pool of Officer Ready Talent'* by Mark A. Pfister

- 34: June 12, 2014 Across The Board newsletter publication: *'Boards and the Baby-Boomer Retirement Effect'* by Mark A. Pfister

- 34a: Harvard Law School Forum on Corporate Governance and Financial Regulation - 'Age Diversity Within Boards of Directors of the S&P 500 Companies' by Annalisa Barrett, Board Governance Research LLC, and Jon Lukomnik, Investor Responsibility Center Institute, April 6, 2017

- 34b: 2016–2017 NACD Public Company Governance Survey

Chapter 13:

- 35: 'The Career Trifecta' from 2017/2018 National Speaking Tour: *'Becoming an Exceptional Board Director Candidate'* by Mark A. Pfister

- 36: Emotional Intelligence Domains & Competencies – 'More Than Sound' HBR *'Emotional Intelligence Has 12 Elements. Which Do You Need to Work On?'* 02/06/17 https://hbr.org/2017/02/emotional-intelligence-has-12 elements-which-do-you-need-to-work-on

- 36a: Mindfulness Intelligence: Bjork Business – An Intelligence System for Leadership Excellence

- 37: 2016–2017 NACD Public Company Governance Survey

- 38: Adapted from the *'Board Candidate'* section - 2017/2018 National Speaking Tour: *'Becoming an Exceptional Board Director Candidate'* by Mark A. Pfister

- 38a: Harvard Law School Forum on Corporate Governance and Financial Regulation - '*2017 Board Diversity Survey*' by Mike Fucci, Deloitte, December 19, 2017

Chapter 14:

- 39: 2016–2017 NACD Public Company Governance Survey

- 40: Ernst & Young's Center for Board Matters created an excellent guide entitled *'Accelerating Board Performance: The Importance of Assessments'* http://www.ey.com/Publication/vwLUAssets/ey-accelerating-board-performance-through-assessments/$File/ey-accelerating-board-performance-through-assessments.pdf

- 39: Adapted from 2017/2018 National Speaking Tour: *'Becoming an Exceptional Board Director Candidate'* by Mark A. Pfister

- 41: NYSE Listing Company Manual, Section 303A.09 http://wallstreet.cch.com/LCMTools/TOCChapter.asp?print=1&manual=/lcm/sections/lcm-

sections/chp_1_4/chp_1_4_3/default.asp&selectedNode= chp_1_4_3

- 42: Wikipedia definition of *'Directors and Officers Liability Insurance'*

- 43: Allianz Global Corporate & Specialty *'Introduction to D&O Insurance'* Risk Briefing – 2010 by Hartmut Mai, Hugo Kidston & Dr. Richard Manson
  http://www.agcs.allianz.com/assets/PDFs/risk%20insig hts/AGCS-DO-infopaper.pdf

- 44: Wikipedia definition of *'Business Judgment Rule'*

- 45: Pearl Meyer's *'2016-2017 Director Compensation Report'* in collaboration with the National Association of Corporate Directors (NACD)

- 46: Spencer Stuart, *'Improving Board Effectiveness,'* January 2012, by Alice Au & Enzo De Angelis

Figure 50: Sphere of Influence / Planes of Congruence Template

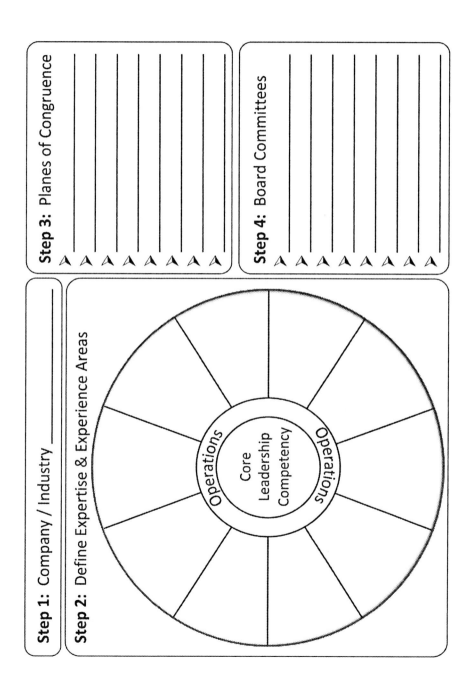

Mark A. Pfister

Special Thanks
for making this book possible

Ulrika 'Red' Nilsson
...For your loving support and understanding during my numerous and recurring *'disappearing acts'* while writing this book. It wasn't you, I promise!...

Michael K. Lorelli
...For being a stand-up guy, a fervent supporter, and a discerning colleague to run Board leadership ideas by. Many thanks for your work and kind words mentioned in the foreword...

Leonard J. Pfister
...For your continuing support, invaluable life coaching, and eagerness to remain as my editor, even when I make updates following *'final'* chapter reviews. I am continually reminded that a son could not have asked for more in a father...

Joe Curio
...For allowing me to plant myself in the back corner of your cigar lounge to write for countless days over numerous long months - and for frequently dropping off water...

Numerous Restaurant / Diner Owners & Waitstaff
...For (generally) allowing me to take up a full booth to write, even across your rush hours. I hope the tips were sufficient...

Thank you.

Mark A. Pfister
www.PfisterStrategy.com